Debbie Mumm's

COUNTRY INSPIRATIONS

More Than 40 Bright and Beautiful Quilt Projects
and Accessories to Fill Your Home with Joy

RODALE

© 2003 Debbie Mumm, Inc.

Debbie Mumm® Creative Teams

Editorial/Project Design
Managing Editors: Carolyn Ogden and Pamela Mostek
Quilt and Craft Designers: Georgie Gerl, Carolyn Lowe, Susan Nelsen, and Jean Van Bockel
Technical Editor: Laura M. Reinstatler
Writers: Pamela Mostek and Darra Williamson
Craft Designer: Jackie Saling
Seamstresses: Candy Huddleston and Nancy Kirkland
Machine Quilters: Pam Clarke, Wanda Jeffries, and Nona King

Book Design and Production
Production Director: Mya Brooks
Graphics Manager: Tom Harlow
Art Directors: Sherry Hassel and Marcia Smith
Graphic Designer: Heather Hughes
Photography: Barros & Barros Photography (Beautiful Butterflies), J. Craig Sweat Photography, and Quad/Photo

Art Team
Senior Artist: Lou McKee
Artists: Kathy Arbuckle, Sandy Ayars, Heather Butler, Kathy Eisenbarth, and Gil-Jin Foster

Marketing/PR
Director of Sales and Marketing: Jeanne Chouteau-Adams

Questions concerning projects and instructions should be directed to Debbie Mumm, Inc., 1116 East Westview Court, Spokane, WA 99218-1384, (888) 819-2923 or (509) 466-3572.

Printed in the United States of America

Rodale Inc. makes every effort to use acid free ∞, recycled paper ♲.

10 9 8 7 6 5 4 3 2 1 hardcover

This material was previously published as *Debbie Mumm's® Country Settings* and *Debbie Mumm's® Birdhouses for Every Season*.
Debbie Mumm's® Country Settings edition published 2000
Debbie Mumm's® Birdhouses for Every Season edition published 2001
Rodale Inc. edition February 2003

Library of Congress Cataloging-in-Publication Data

Mumm, Debbie.
    Debbie Mumm's country inspirations : more than 40 bright and beautiful quilt projects and accessories to fill your home with joy / Debbie Mumm.
        p.   cm.
    ISBN 1–57954–694–3   hardcover
    1. Patchwork—Patterns.   2. Quilting—Patterns.
I. Title: Country inspirations.   II. Title.
TT835 M824978   2003
746.46—dc21   2002036873

RODALE

WE INSPIRE AND ENABLE PEOPLE TO IMPROVE
THEIR LIVES AND THE WORLD AROUND THEM

TABLE of CONTENTS

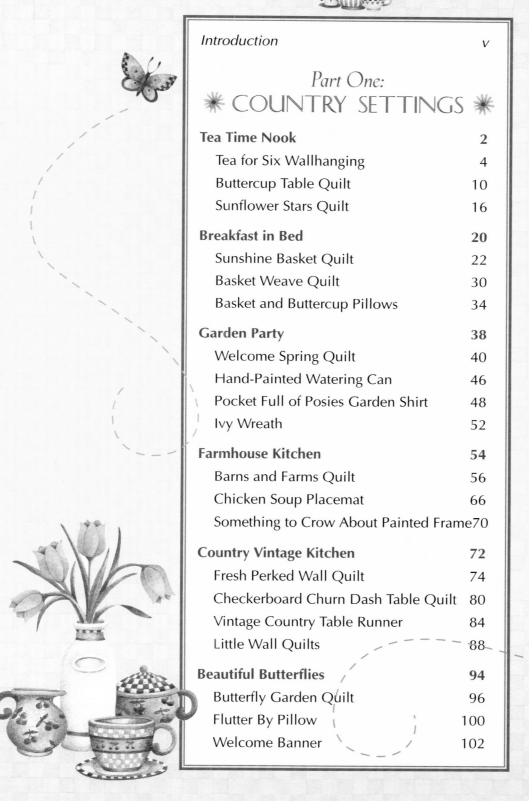

Part Two:
BIRDHOUSES FOR EVERY SEASON

I love to decorate with quilts! Using quilts in every setting adds color, character, texture, and warmth to every room of your home. I also use quilts outdoors for special occasions. What could be more wonderful than combining the beauty and intricacy of a pieced quilt and a glorious garden setting? In this special book combining my favorite country looks and popular birdhouse projects, you'll find beautiful quilts for every setting and every season. From seasonal birdhouse quilts to quilts featuring a variety of country decorating themes, this book has a wealth of projects from which to choose!

Discover lots of quilting inspiration in the first part of the book called Country Settings. From glorious quilts for a garden room to a country vintage kitchen filled with nostalgic red, yellow, and blue quilts, to a bedroom resplendent in sunny quilting creations, Country Settings offers 20 projects to help you decorate your country home.

Birdhouses for Every Season, the second part of the book, will transport you to a whimsical world of birds, butterflies, and blossoms. Select from more than 25 projects to bring the fanciful feeling of a garden to every room in your home. From a Trellis in Bloom Bed Quilt in spring to a Birdhouse Sampler in summer and from a Fall Flight Quilt to a wintry Crimson Cardinals Table Quilt, you'll find the perfect project for every setting in your home. Whimsical and wonderful artwork adds a touch of magic to this delightful book. I know it will make browsing through your book all the more pleasurable as you turn each page to discover even more country inspiration.

Enjoy!

Debbie Mumm

Debbie Mumm's®
COUNTRY SETTINGS

Step into these warm and inviting settings created by this gathering of delightful quilts. From vintage country kitchens to lovely garden patios ~ you'll find many new ideas for decorating your home with charming wallhangings, cheery table quilts, colorful tablerunners, placemats, cozy lap quilts, plus much more.

TEA TIME NOOK

Take a few moments out of your busy day to rest and reflect with a cup of warm tea. It's a well-deserved treat just for you. There's just something inviting about a cup of tea ... especially in your own delightful tea time nook. Set your table with a lovely quilt topped with your favorite tea set ... the personal touches that will make your tea party a special occasion.

TEAPOTS DINNERWARE

TEA FOR SIX

WALLHANGING

Finished Size: 29" square

Photo: page 2

DECLARE YOUR FONDNESS FOR TEA

with this charming, colorful wallhanging. Bold letters spell it out for all to see while delicate teacups await your pleasure. You'll be delighted with the quick-pieced construction. Why not celebrate with a rainy-day party for five of your closest quilting friends? Read all instructions before beginning and use ¼"-wide seams throughout.

Quilt Layout

FABRIC REQUIREMENTS

Directional fabrics are not recommended.

Fabric A *(cups, saucers, and handles)*
10" square each of six fabrics

Fabric B *(background)* - ¾ yard

Fabric C *(letters)* - ¼ yard

Accent Border - ⅙ yard

Border - ⅜ yard

Backing - 1 yard

Binding - ⅜ yard

Lightweight batting - 33" square

CUTTING THE STRIPS AND PIECES

Pre-wash and press fabrics. Using rotary cutter, see-through ruler, and cutting mat, cut the following strips and pieces. If indicated, some will need to be cut again into smaller strips and pieces. The approximate width of the fabric is 42".

Measurements for all pieces include ¼"-wide seam allowance.

Fabric A

From each 10" square, cut

* One 5½" square *(teacups)*

* One 1½" x 5½" rectangle *(saucers)*

Fabric B *(background)*

* Four 1½" x 21½" strips

* One 1½" x 22½" strip

* Two 2½" x 42" strips, cut into
  * Seven 2½" x 6½" pieces
  * Two 2½" x 5½" pieces
  * Two 2½" x 3½" pieces
  * One 2½" x 1½" piece

* Two 1½" x 42" strips, cut into
  * Four 1½" x 6½" pieces
  * One 1½" x 4½" piece
  * One 1½" x 3½" piece
  * Twenty-six 1½" squares

Fabric C *(letters)*

* Two 1½" x 42" strips, cut into
  * Three 1½" x 6½" pieces
  * Two 1½" x 5½" pieces
  * One 1½" x 4½" piece
  * One 1½" x 3½" piece
  * Two 1½" x 2½" pieces
  * Twelve 1½" squares

* One 2½" x 5½" piece

Accent Border

* Four 1" x 42" strips

Border

* Four 3" x 42" strips

Backing

* One 33" square

Binding

* Four 2¾" x 42" strips

MAKING THE BLOCKS

You'll be making six Teacup Blocks and three alphabet blocks, one each for the letters "T," "E," and "A."

Whenever possible, use the assembly line method for each step. Position pieces with right sides together and line up next to your sewing machine. Stitch the first unit together then continue sewing others without breaking threads. When all units are sewn, clip threads to separate them. Press in direction of arrows in diagrams.

TEACUP BLOCKS

For all blocks, refer to Quick Corner Triangle directions on page 216. Block will measure 6½" x 7½".

1. **Cup Unit:** Sew a 1½" Fabric B square to two adjacent corners of a 5½" Fabric A square. Press. Make a total of six.

A = 5½ x 5½
B = 1½ x 1½
Make 6

2. **Saucer Unit:** Sew a 1½" Fabric B square to each end of a 1½" x 5½" Fabric A rectangle. Press. Make a total of six.

A = 1½ x 5½
B = 1½ x 1½
Make 6

3. Sew a cup unit from step 1 to a contrasting-color saucer unit from step 2. Press toward saucer. Make a total of six.

Make 6

CREATE YOUR OWN CENTERPIECE

Who says a teapot is just for serving tea? With a few added touches, it can be magically transformed into a charming centerpiece for your tea table.

For a look at the delightful teapots designed by Debbie Mumm®, see the color photo on page 2. Once you've picked just the right one, the next step is to add your personal touch to it.

How about filling it with delightful flowers from your garden … bright yellow daffodils in the spring or sunny zinnias in the summer. If your garden isn't in bloom, try filling your teapot with a pot of ivy-the perfect finishing touch to your tea party.

4. Refer to Hand Appliqué directions on page 216. Trace cup handle from pattern on page 8, using Fabric A scraps. Position a contrasting color handle for each teacup and appliqué to 2½" x 6½" Fabric B piece, referring to project layout on page 6 for placement.

5. Sew unit from step 4 to right side of each cup-and-saucer unit. Press. Make a total of six.

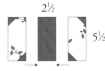

Make 6

ALPHABET BLOCKS

LETTER "T":

1. Sew two 1½" Fabric C squares to opposite corners of each 2½" x 5½" Fabric B piece. Press. Make one of each following diagrams.

B = 2½ x 5½
C = 1½ x 1½
Make 1 of each

2. Sew 2½" x 5½" Fabric C piece between units from step 1. Press.

3. Sew one 1½" x 6½" Fabric C piece and one 1½" x 6½" Fabric B piece to unit from step 2. Press. Block will measure 6½" x 7½".

LETTER "E":

1. Sew a 1½" Fabric C square to each end of a 1½" x 6½" Fabric B piece. Press.

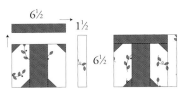

B = 1½ x 6½
C = 1½ x 1½

2. Repeat step 1 to sew a 1½" Fabric C square to each end of 1½" x 4½" Fabric B piece. Press.

B = 1½ x 4½
C = 1½ x 1½

3. Sew the 1½" x 3½" Fabric C piece between the 1½" x 3½" Fabric B piece and one 2½" x 3½" Fabric B piece. Press.

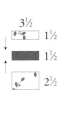

4. Sew unit from step 3 between 1½" x 4½" Fabric C piece and unit from step 2. Press.

5. Sew unit from step 4 between two 1½" x 5½" Fabric C pieces. Press.

6. Sew unit from step 5 between one 1½" x 6½" Fabric B piece and the unit from step 1. Press. Block will measure 6½" x 7½".

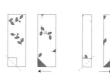

LETTER "A":

1. Sew a 1½" Fabric B square to one end of remaining 1½" x 6½" Fabric C pieces. Make one each following diagrams. Press.

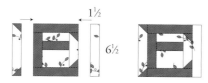

B = 1½ x 1½
C = 1½ x 6½
Make 1 of each

2. Repeat step 1 to sew one 1½" Fabric C square to a 2½" x 6½" Fabric B piece and to remaining 1½" x 6½" Fabric B piece. Press.

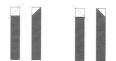

B = 2½ x 6½
   1½ x 6½
C = 1½ x 1½
Make 1 of each

3. Sew a 1½" Fabric C square to adjacent corners of a remaining 2½" x 3½" Fabric B piece. Press.

B = 2½ x 3½
C = 1½ x 1½

4. Sew 2½" x 1½" Fabric B piece between two 2½" x 1½" Fabric C pieces. Press.

5. Arrange and sew units from steps 1–4 as shown. Press. Block will measure 6½" x 7½".

ASSEMBLY

1. Referring to project layout on page 4, arrange one horizontal row of alphabet blocks (to spell TEA) and two horizontal rows of three Teacup Blocks. Sew blocks into rows. Press.

2. Arrange and sew together 1½" x 21½" Fabric B strips, Teacup rows, and Alphabet row as shown. Press.

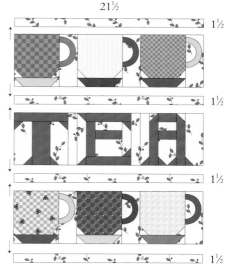

3. Sew 1½" x 22½" Fabric B strip to left side of unit. Press.

BORDERS

1. Measure quilt through center from side to side. Trim two 1" x 42" accent border strips to this measurement. Sew to top and bottom of quilt top. Press toward accent border.

2. Measure quilt through center from top to bottom, including accent border. Trim remaining 1" x 42" accent border strips to this measurement. Sew to sides. Press.

3. Repeat measuring as described in step 1. Cut two 3" x 42" border strips to this measurement and sew to top and bottom. Press toward outside border.

4. Repeat measuring as described in step 2. Cut remaining 3" x 42" border strips to this measurement. Sew to sides. Press.

LAYERING AND FINISHING

1. Arrange and baste backing, batting, and top together, referring to Layering the Quilt directions on page 217.

2. Hand or machine quilt as desired.

3. Refer to Binding the Quilt directions on page 217, and use 2¾" x 42" strips for binding.

A NOTE FROM DEBBIE . . .

Sharing our hearts
and a cup of tea
With friends is always a
special time.

Why not call a friend
and plan
To have tea this very week!
Whether at home or in your
favorite tearoom,
make some time
and make some memories
together.

Love, Debbie

from the book
Tea Time Friends
Brownlow©1999
illustrated by Debbie Mumm®

cup handle
trace 6

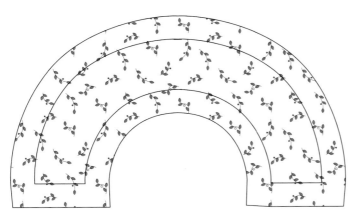

TEAPOTS DINNERWARE

This festive dinnerware invites friends and family to the table for an afternoon of warm scones and tea. For information on where to buy Debbie Mumm® dinnerware, visit www.debbiemumm.com or call (888) 819-2923.

BUTTERCUP

TABLE QUILT

Finished Size: 65" square

Photo: page 9

BREEZY BUTTERCUPS,

LATTICE-LIKE SASHING,

a maze of crisp, crisscrossing garden paths. No matter the season, it feels like summer when this cheerful quilt graces your table. Read all instructions before beginning and use ¼"-wide seams throughout.

Quilt Layout

FABRIC REQUIREMENTS

Directional fabrics are not recommended.

Fabric A *(buttercups)* - ⅓ yard each of six different fabrics

Fabric B *(buttercup backgrounds)* ⅓ yard each of four different fabrics

Fabric C *(buttercup centers)* Twenty-four 1½" squares from assorted scraps

Fabric D *(corner, chain, and partial chain blocks)* - ¼ yard each of four different fabrics

Fabric E *(chain background)* 1¾ yards

Inside Accent Borders - ⅙ yard each of three different fabrics

Sashing - ⅞ yard

Outside Accent Border - ¼ yard

Border - ¾ yard

Binding - ⅔ yard

Backing - 4 yards

Lightweight batting - 69" square

CUTTING THE STRIPS AND PIECES

Read first paragraph of Cutting the Strips and Pieces on page 5.

Fabric A (buttercups)

* Two 3½" x 42" strips, cut into
  * Sixteen 3½" x 2½" pieces
  * Eight 3½" x 1½" pieces
* One 1½" x 42" strip, cut into
  * Eight 1½" squares

Repeat for each of six fabrics.

Fabric B (buttercup backgrounds)

* Two 2½" x 42" strips, cut into
  * Twenty-four 2½" squares
* Two 1½" x 42" strips, cut into
  * Forty-eight 1½" squares

Repeat for each of four fabrics.

Fabric D (corner squares, chain, and partial chain blocks)

* Three 1½" x 27" strips
* One 1½" x 6" piece, cut into
  * Three 1½" squares

Repeat for each of four fabrics.

Fabric E (chain background)

* Two 6½" x 42" strips, cut into
  * Twelve 6½" squares
* Two 3½" x 42" strips, cut into
  * Twelve 3½" x 6½" pieces

* Two 4½" x 27" strips
* Six 2½" x 27" strips
* Four 1½" x 27" strips
* One 1½" x 42" strip, cut into
  * Eight 1½" x 2½" pieces
  * Eight 1½" squares

Inside Accent Borders

* Four 1" x 42" strips

Repeat for each of three fabrics.

Sashing

* Six 1½" x 42" strips
* Nine 1½" x 42" strips, cut into
  * Four 1½" x 39½" strips
  * Twenty-four 1½" x 7½" pieces

Outside Accent Border

* Six 1" x 42" strips

Border

* Seven 3½" x 42" strips

Binding

* Eight 2¾" x 42" strips

MAKING THE BLOCKS

You will be making twenty-four Buttercup Blocks, four Corner Blocks, thirteen Chain Blocks, and eight Partial Chain Blocks. Each Buttercup Block pairs a single Fabric A and Fabric B and has a scrappy Fabric C center. The block will measure 7½" square. The Corner, Chain, and Partial Chain Blocks combine a variety of medium fabrics (Fabric D) with a consistent light background (Fabric E).

The size of the Corner Block is 3½" square; the Chain Block, 6½" square; and the Partial Chain Block, 6½" x 3½".

Whenever possible, use the assembly line method for each step. Position pieces right sides together and line up next to your sewing machine. Stitch first unit together, then continue sewing others without breaking threads. When all units are sewn, clip threads to separate them. Press in direction of arrows in diagrams.

BUTTERCUP BLOCKS

For all blocks, refer to Quick Corner Triangle directions on page 216.

1. For each block, sew one 1½" Fabric C square between two matching 1½" Fabric A squares. Press. Make a total of twenty-four.

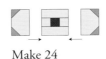

Make 24

2. Sew unit from step 1 between two matching 3½" x 1½" Fabric A pieces. Press. Make a total of twenty-four.

3½
1½
Make 24

3. Refer to Quick Corner Triangle directions on page 216. For each block, sew two matching 1½" Fabric B squares to each of four matching 3½" x 2½" Fabric A pieces. Press. Make a total of ninety-six.

A = 3½ x 2½
B = 1½ x 1½
Make 96

4. For each block, sew unit from step 3 between two matching 2½" Fabric B squares. Press. Make a total of forty-eight.

2½
2½
Make 48

5. Sew unit from step 2 between two matching units from step 3. Press. Make a total of twenty-four.

Make 24

6. For each block, sew unit from step 5 between two matching units from step 4. Press. Make a total of twenty-four. Block will measure 7½" square.

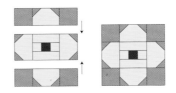

CORNER BLOCKS

1. Sew one 1½" Fabric D square between two 1½" Fabric E squares. Press. Make a total of four.

1½
1½
Make 4

2. Sew one 1½" Fabric D square to one 1½" x 2½" Fabric E piece. Press. Make a total of eight.

2½   1½
1½
Make 8

3. Sew unit from step 1 between two units from step 2. Press. Make a total of four. Block will measure 3½" square.

Make 4

CHAIN AND PARTIAL CHAIN BLOCKS

1. Sew two different 1½" x 27" Fabric D strips together lengthwise. Sew one 2½" x 27" Fabric E strip to each side as shown. Repeat to make two strip sets. Press. Using rotary cutter and ruler, cut seventeen 1½" segments from each strip set for a total of thirty-four segments.

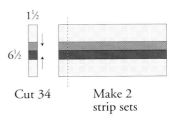

1½
6½
Cut 34   Make 2 strip sets

2. Sew one 2½" x 27" Fabric E strip between two different 1½" x 27" Fabric D strips and two 1½" x 27" Fabric E strips. Repeat to make two strip sets. Press. Cut seventeen 1½" segments from each strip set for a total of thirty-four segments.

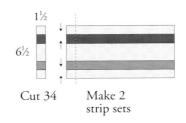

1½
6½
Cut 34   Make 2 strip sets

3. Sew one 4½" x 27" Fabric E strip between two different 1½" x 27" Fabric D strips. Repeat to make two strip sets. Press. Cut a total of seventeen 1½" segments from each strip set for a total of thirty-four segments.

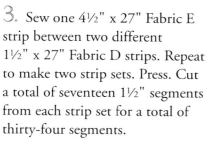

Cut 34   Make 2 strip sets

4. For each Chain Block, sew two different units from step 1 between two units each from steps 2 and 3 as shown. Press. Make a total of thirteen. Block will measure 6½" square.

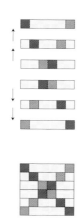

Make 13

5. For each Partial Chain Block, sew one unit from step 2 between one unit from step 1 and one unit from step 3. Press. Make a total of eight. Block will measure 6½" x 3½".

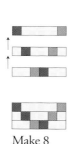

Make 8

ASSEMBLY

1. Arrange two Corner Blocks, two Partial Chain Blocks, and three 3½" x 6½" Fabric E pieces in a horizontal row as shown. Sew and press. Make two rows.

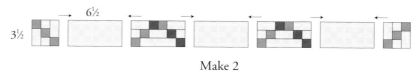

Make 2

2. Arrange three Chain Blocks, two 3½" x 6½" Fabric E pieces, and two 6½" Fabric E squares in a horizontal row. Sew and press. Make three rows.

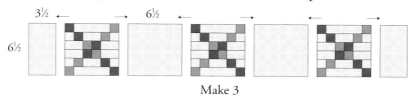

Make 3

3. Arrange two Chain Blocks, three 6½" Fabric E squares, and two Partial Chain Blocks in a horizontal row. Sew and press. Make two rows.

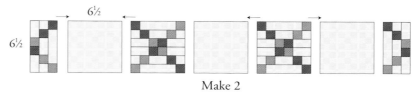

Make 2

4. Referring to project layout on page 12, arrange rows in correct order. Join rows and press. Center unit will measure 36½" square.

 **BORDERS**

1. Measure quilt through center from side to side. Trim two matching 1" x 42" inside accent border strips to this measurement. Sew to top and bottom. Press toward accent border.

2. Measure quilt through center from top to bottom, including border. Trim remaining matching 1" x 42" inside accent border strips to this measurement. Sew to sides. Press.

3. Repeat steps 1 and 2 to add second set of matching top, bottom, and side inside accent border strips to quilt. Press.

4. Repeat steps 1 and 2 to add third set of matching top, bottom, and side inside accent border strips to quilt. Press.

5. Lay out a pleasing arrangement of five Buttercup Blocks alternating with four 1½" x 7½" sashing strips. Sew and press. Make two rows.

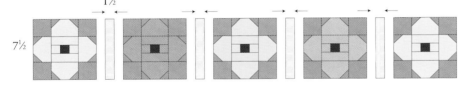

Make 2

6. Sew 1½" x 39½" sashing strips to top and bottom edges of pieced rows from step 5. Press toward sashing strips.

7. Sew sashed rows from step 6 to top and bottom of quilt. Press toward sashed rows.

8. Lay out a pleasing arrangement of seven Buttercup Blocks alternating with eight 1½" x 7½" sashing strips. Sew and press. Make two rows.

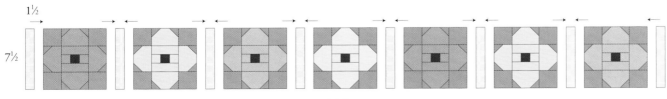

Make 2

9. Sew remaining 1½" x 42" sashing strips together to make one continuous 1½"-wide strip. From this strip, cut four 1½" x 57½" sashing strips. Sew sashing strips to top and bottom edges of pieced rows from step 8. Press toward sashing strips.

10. Sew sashed rows from step 9 to sides of quilt. Press toward sashed rows.

11. Sew 1" x 42" outside accent border strips together to make one continuous 1"-wide strip. Measure and cut two outside accent border strips as in step 1. Sew to top and bottom. Press toward sashing strips.

12. Measure and cut two 1"-wide outside accent border strips as in step 2. Sew to sides. Press.

13. Sew 3½" x 42" border strips together to make one continuous 3½"-wide strip. Repeat steps 11 and 12 to fit, trim, and sew 3½"-wide border strips to top, bottom, and sides of quilt. Press toward border.

1. Cut backing fabric crosswise into two equal pieces. Sew pieces together to make one 72" x 84" (approximate) backing piece. Arrange and baste backing, batting, and top together referring to Layering the Quilt directions on page 217.

2. Hand or machine quilt as desired.

3. Sew 2¾" x 42" binding strips together in pairs. Refer to Binding the Quilt directions on page 217 to finish.

FOR A PERFECT ACCENT ...

... create tea napkins to coordinate with your Buttercup Table Quilt. Choose a luscious shade of yellow to match the array of buttercups on the quilt, or choose a color that is a perfect complement to your own tea time nook. They are a quick and easy project that will give that special personal touch to your tea table.

For each napkin you will need:

- One 12½" square of fabric (napkin)
- One 13½" square of fabric (napkin)
- Two 1" x 12½" strips (contrasting trim)
- Two 1" x 13 ½" strips (contrasting trim)

To make the napkin:

- Sew the two 1" x 12½" strips on the top and bottom of the 12½" square. Press toward napkin. Sew the 1" x 13½" strips to the sides. Press.

- Position the unit from step 1 and the 13½" square with right sides together. Using a ¼" inch seam, sew around all four sides, leaving a 2" opening on one side for turning.

- Turn right side out and press.

- Hand stitch side opening closed.

- Repeat for each napkin.

SUN FLOWER STARS QUILT

Finished Size: 43" square

Photo: page 2

WHETHER DRAPED OVER A TABLE,

cupboard, or buffet, this sunny topper adds special-occasion sparkle to even the most casual family mealtime. Star-inspired sunflowers dance around a large center panel— the perfect showcase for a favorite fabric. Read all instructions before beginning and use ¼"-wide seams throughout.

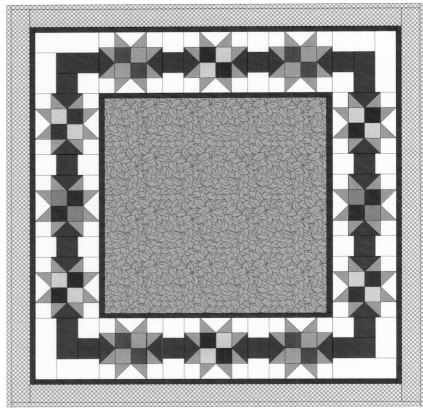

Quilt Layout

FABRIC REQUIREMENTS

Fabric A (*sunflower petals*) - ⅓ yard

Fabric B (*background*) - ⅔ yard

Fabric C (*vine spacer and vine corner blocks*) - ⅜ yard

Fabric D (*sunflower centers*)
One 2" x 10" strip each of twelve different fabrics

Center Square - ⅔ yard

Inside Accent Border - ¼ yard

Outside Accent Border - ¼ yard

Border - ⅓ yard

Binding - ½ yard

Backing - 2⅝ yard

Lightweight batting - 47" square

CUTTING THE STRIPS AND PIECES

Read first paragraph of Cutting the Strips and Pieces on page 5.

Fabric A *(sunflower petals)*
* Five 2" x 42" strips, cut into
  • Ninety-six 2" squares

Fabric B *(background)*
* Two 2½" x 42" strips *(vine spacer blocks)*
* Two 2½" x 42" strips, cut into
  • Four 2½" x 6½" pieces *(vine corner blocks)*
  • Four 2½" x 4½" pieces *(vine corner blocks)*
  • Four 2½" squares *(vine corner blocks)*
* Five 2" x 42" strips, cut into
  • Twenty-four 2" x 3½" pieces *(sunflower blocks)*
  • Forty-eight 2" squares *(sunflower blocks)*

Fabric C
* One 2½" x 42" strip *(vine spacer blocks)*
* One 2½" x 42" strip, cut into
  • Four 2½" x 4½" pieces *(vine corner blocks)*
  • Four 2½" squares *(vine corner blocks)*

* Three 2" x 42" strips, cut into
  • Twenty-four 2" x 3½" pieces *(sunflower blocks)*

Center Square
* One 22½" square

Inside Accent Border
* Two 1½" x 24½" strips
* Two 1½" x 22½" strips

Outside Accent Border
* Four 1½" x 42" strips

Border
* Four 2½" x 42" strips

Binding
* Five 2¾" x 42" strips

* *Delightful Debbie Mumm® teapots can be a colorful accent to your home with her wallpaper border from Imperial Home Décor Group. Call (800) 539-5399 or visit www.imp-wall.com.*

MAKING THE BLOCKS

You'll be making twelve Sunflower Blocks, eight Vine Spacer Blocks, and four Vine Corner Blocks.

Whenever possible, use the assembly-line method for each step. Position pieces with right sides together and line up next to your sewing machine. Stitch the first unit together, then continue sewing others without breaking threads. When all units are sewn, clip threads to separate them. Press in direction of arrows in diagrams.

SUNFLOWER BLOCKS

I. Sew 2" x 10" Fabric D strips together in pairs to make six strip sets. Press seams toward darker fabrics. Using rotary cutter and ruler, cut four 2"-wide segments from each strip set.

2

3½

Cut 4   Make 6 strip sets

2. Sew matching segments together in pairs as shown to make twelve four-patch units. Press.

Make 12

3. Refer to Quick Corner Triangle directions on page 216. Sew one 2" Fabric A square to each 2" x 3½" Fabric B rectangle as shown. Press. Make a total of twenty-four.

A= 2 x 2
B= 2 x 3½
Make 24

4. Sew a second 2" Fabric A square to each unit from step 3. Press.

A/B = 2 x 3½
Make 24

5. Repeat steps 3 and 4 to sew two 2" Fabric A squares to each 2" x 3½" Fabric C rectangle. Press. Make a total of twenty-four.

Make 24

6. Sew one unit from step 4 between two 2" Fabric B squares. Press. Make a total of twenty-four.

Make 24

7. Sew one four-patch unit from step 2 between two units from step 5. Press. Make a total of twelve.

Make 12

8. Sew units from step 7 between two units from step 6 as shown. Press. Make a total of twelve. Block will measure 6½" square.

Make 12

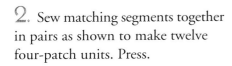 VINE BLOCKS

1. For Vine Spacer Blocks, sew one 2½" x 42" Fabric C strip between two 2½" x 42" Fabric B strips to make a strip set. Press toward Fabric C. Cut eight 3½"-wide segments.

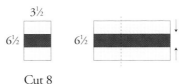

Cut 8

2. For Vine Corner Squares, sew 2½" Fabric B and 2½" Fabric C squares together in pairs. Make a total of four. Press.

Make 4

3. Sew 2½" x 4½" Fabric C rectangles to units from step 2. Make four. Press toward Fabric C rectangles.

Make 4

4. Sew 2½" x 4½" Fabric B rectangles to units from step 3. Make a total of four. Press toward step 3 unit.

Make 4

5. Sew 2½" x 6½" Fabric B rectangles to units from step 4. Make a total of four. Press.

Make 4

 ASSEMBLY

1. Sew 1½" x 22½" inside accent border strips to top and bottom of 22½" center square. Press toward accent border. Sew 1½" x 24½" inside accent border strips to sides of center square. Press.

2. Arrange and sew together three Sunflower and two Vine Spacer Blocks to make four rows. Press seam allowances toward vine spacer blocks.

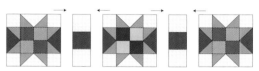

Make 4

3. Fit, pin, and sew one row each from step 2 to top and bottom of quilt. Press toward accent border.

4. Referring to quilt diagram on page 16, sew 6½" Vine Corner Squares to each end of remaining rows. Press toward corner squares. Fit, pin, and sew to sides. Press.

5. Measure quilt through center from side to side. Trim two 1½"-wide outside accent border strips to this measurement. Sew to top and bottom. Press toward accent border.

6. Measure quilt through center from top to bottom, including accent borders. Trim remaining 1½"-wide outside accent border strips to this measurement. Sew to sides. Press.

7. Sew 2½" x 42" border strips end to end to make one continuous 2½"-wide strip.

8. Repeat measuring as described in step 5. Cut two 2½"-wide strips to this measurement from border strip. Sew to top and bottom of quilt. Press seams toward outside border.

9. Repeat measuring as described in step 6. Cut two strips to this measurement from remaining 2½"-wide border strip. Sew to sides. Press.

 LAYERING AND FINISHING

1. Cut backing fabric crosswise into two equal pieces. Sew pieces together to make one 47" x 84" (approximate) backing piece. Arrange and baste backing, batting, and top together, referring to Layering the Quilt directions on page 217.

2. Hand or machine quilt as desired.

3. Refer to Binding the Quilt directions on page 217, and use 2¾" x 42" strips to finish.

BREAKFAST IN BED

Imagine a luxurious Sunday morning. The warm sun is spilling through your bedroom window, and you have all the time in the world to enjoy it. You are relaxing in your bed that is adorned with a sunshine-colored quilt and mountains of soft pillows.

For an added treat, you have just been served a breakfast of fresh walnut scones and raspberry tea in your favorite fanciful teacup. What a perfect setting. Can a day that starts this way be anything less than wonderful?

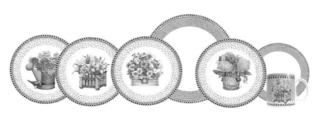

SPRING BOUQUET DINNERWARE

21

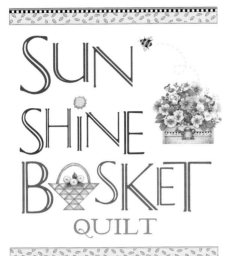

SUNSHINE BASKET QUILT

Finished Size: 49" square

Photo: page 29

WHAT COULD BE A MORE PERFECT

welcome for spring than a delicate pastel basket brimming with pretty posies? Graceful waving vines and a ring of sweet little baskets create a springtime mood. Tossed over the Basket Weave Quilt and coupled with a delightful pillow or two, this sunshine quilt dresses any bedtop in romantic style. Read all instructions before beginning and use ¼"-wide seams throughout.

Quilt Layout

FABRIC REQUIREMENTS

Fabric A *(background)* - 2 yards

Fabric B *(center basket block)* ⅝ yard

Fabric C *(center basket block)* ⅝ yard

Fabric D *(corner flower blocks)* ⅛ yard

Fabric E *(corner flower block centers)* Four 1½" squares

Fabric F *(small basket blocks)* ⅓ yard each of four different fabrics

First Accent Border - ⅛ yard

Appliqué Flowers - ⅛ yard or assorted scraps

Appliqué Flower Centers assorted scraps

Leaves - ⅛ yard or assorted scraps

Vines - ⅓ yard

Inside Setting Triangles One 8¾" square

Second Accent Border - ⅙ yard

Outside Setting Triangles - ⅝ yard

Third Accent Border - ¼ yard

Backing - 3 yards

Binding - ½ yard

Lightweight batting - 53" square

CUTTING THE STRIPS AND PIECES

Read first paragraph of Cutting the Strips and Pieces on page 5.

Fabric A (background)

* One 10⅞" square
* Four 4½" x 42" strips cut into
  * Twenty-eight 4½" squares
* Three 3½" x 42" strips, cut into
  * Eight 3½" x 12½" pieces
* Eleven 2½" x 42" strips, cut into
  * One 2½" x 14½" piece
  * Two 2½" x 10½" pieces
  * One 2½" x 8½" piece
  * One hundred fifty-three 2½" squares
* One 1½" x 42" strip, cut into
  * Sixteen 1½" squares

Fabric B (center flower basket)

* One 18" square, cut into
  * One 1" x 24" bias strip
* One 2½" x 22" strip, cut into
  * Eight 2½" squares

Fabric C (center flower basket)

* One 18" square, cut into
  * One 1" x 24" bias strip
* Two 4" squares
* Three 2½" squares

Fabric D (corner flower blocks)

* One 1½" x 42" strip, cut into
  * Eight 1½" x 3½" pieces
  * Eight 1½" squares

Fabric F (small basket blocks)

* One 4½" x 42" strip, cut into
  * Seven 4½" squares
* One 2½" x 42" strip, cut into
  * Fourteen 2½" squares

Repeat for each of four fabrics.

First Accent Border

* Two 1½" x 42" strips, cut into
  * Two 1½" x 16½" pieces
  * Two 1½" x 14½" pieces

Vines

* Two 10" squares, cut into
  * Eight 1" x 12" bias strips

Second Accent Border

* Four 1¼" x 42" strips

Outside Setting Triangles

* Two 18¼" squares

Third Accent Border

* Four 1½" x 42" strips

Binding

* Five 2¾" x 42" strips

DISPLAYING YOUR SUNSHINE QUILT

Our Sunshine Basket Quilt is a delightful topper for our Basket Weave Quilt shown on page 20.

Not only will it bring a touch of sunshine to your bedroom, it can also add whimsy and color to other spots in your home too. Try it in the middle of your dining room table, your sideboard, or your buffet. Its delicate appliquéd flowers and pieced baskets are sure to bring compliments from the guests at your next dinner party.

Or try it hanging on point in a special spot in your living room or entryway. It becomes an eye-catching wall quilt. Anywhere it's displayed, it will add just the right personal touch to your home.

 MAKING THE BLOCKS

You will be making one Center Basket Block, four Corner Flower Blocks for the inside setting-triangle units, and twenty-eight Small Basket Blocks for the border.

Whenever possible, use the assembly line method for each step. Position pieces right sides together and line up next to your sewing machine. Stitch first unit together, then continue sewing others without breaking threads. When all units are sewn, clip threads to separate them. Press in direction of arrows in diagrams.

 CENTER BASKET BLOCK

For all blocks, refer to Quick Corner Triangle directions on page 216.

1. Using 2½" Fabric A and Fabric B squares, make eight units. Press. Repeat, using 2½" Fabric A and Fabric C squares to make three units.

A = 2½ x 2½   A = 2½ x 2½
B = 2½ x 2½   C = 2½ x 2½
Make 8   Make 3

2. Cut each 4" Fabric C square twice diagonally to make eight triangles.

3. Arrange 2½" Fabric A squares, A/C and A/B units from step 1, and Fabric C quarter-square triangles into four rows as shown. Sew into rows. Press.

4. Join rows, carefully matching seams. Press. Add two Fabric C quarter-square triangles to finish unit as shown. Press.

5. Cut 10⅞" Fabric A square in half once diagonally to make two triangles. Sew one triangle to unit from step 4. Press.

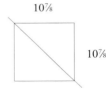

10⅞

10⅞

6. Sew one A/B unit from step 1 to 2½" x 8½" Fabric A piece. Press.

8½

2½

7. Sew unit from step 5 between unit from step 6 and one 2½" x 10½" Fabric A piece. Press.

10½
2½
10½

8. Sew remaining A/B unit between 2½" Fabric A square and 2½" x 10½" Fabric A piece. Press.

2½
10½

9. Sew unit from step 7 between 2½" x 14½" Fabric A piece and unit from step 8. Press. Block will measure 14½" square.

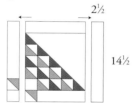

2½
14½

10. Sew 1½" x 14½" first accent border strips to opposite sides of block. Press seams toward accent border. Sew 1½" x 16½" first accent border strips to remaining two sides. Press.

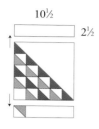 FLOWER BASKET APPLIQUÉ

1. For basket handles, fold 1" x 24" Fabric B bias strip right sides together. Stitch along unfinished edge to make ¼" bias tube. Turn and press with ¼" bias bar. Repeat for 1" x 24" Fabric C bias strip.

2. Refer to Hand Appliqué directions on page 216. Position Fabric B and Fabric C bias strips side by side and machine baste across one pair of short raw edges to secure. Weave strips into a "braid" and stitch across raw edges to secure.

3. Refer to project layout on page 24 to position braided handle above basket with short raw edges overlapping seam. Machine or hand stitch handle in place, opening seams as necessary to insert raw edges of handle. Restitch seams. Press.

4. Refer to Hand Appliqué directions on page 216. Use appliqué patterns on page 28 to make templates for flower, flower center, and leaf. Trace six flowers on flower fabric, six flower centers on flower center fabric, and nine leaves on leaf fabric. Cut out appliqués, adding ¼" seam allowance around each piece.

5. Refer to project layout on page 22 to arrange flowers, flower centers, and leaves in basket. Appliqué in place.

 CORNER FLOWER BLOCKS

1. Sew one 1½" Fabric E square between two 1½" Fabric D squares. Press. Make a total of four.

1½
1½
Make 4

2. Refer to Quick Corner Triangle directions on 216. Sew two 1½" Fabric A squares to each 1½" x 3½" Fabric D piece. Press. Make a total of eight.

A = 1½ x 1½
D = 1½ x 3½
Make 8

3. Sew one unit from step 1 between two units from step 2. Press. Make a total of four. Block will measure 3½" square.

Make 4

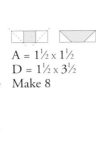

CORNER TRIANGLES

1. Cut 8¾" square in half twice diagonally to make four inside setting triangles. Sew one 3½" x 12½" Fabric A strip to one short side of each triangle, aligning straight edges at corner. Press seams toward triangle.

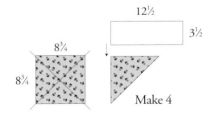

12½
3½
8¾
8¾
Make 4

2. Sew Corner Flower Blocks to one end of each remaining 3½" x 12½" Fabric A strip. Press seams toward Corner Blocks. Make a total of four.

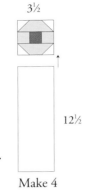

3½
12½
Make 4

3. Sew units from step 2 to units from step 1 as shown, aligning straight edges at corners. Press seams toward triangles. Make a total of four.

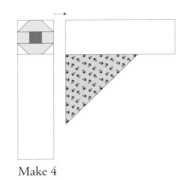

Make 4

4. Trim "tails" of Fabric A strips even with long raw edge of setting triangles.

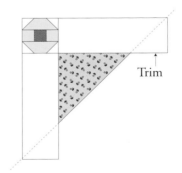

Trim

5. Sew one pieced corner triangle to each side of bordered center block. Press seams toward block accent border.

6. For vines, fold each 1" x 12" bias strip right sides together. Stitch along unfinished edge to make ¼" bias tube. Turn and press with ¼" bias bar. Make eight.

7. Refer to project layout on page 24. Position one ¼" x 12" bias vine on each Fabric A strip (two per corner), with vine's short raw edges overlapping seams. Machine or hand stitch vines in place, opening seams as necessary to insert raw edges of vine. Restitch seams. Press.

8. Refer to Hand Appliqué directions on page 216. Use leaf template to trace sixteen additional leaves on leaf fabric. Cut out appliqués, adding ¼" seam allowance around each piece.

9. Refer to project layout on page 22 to position two leaves along each appliquéd vine from step 7. Appliqué in place.

SMALL BASKET BLOCKS

1. Refer to Quick Corner Triangle directions on page 216. Using 2½" Fabric A and Fabric F squares, make fifty-six units. Press.

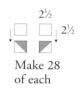

A = 2½ x 2½
F = 2½ x 2½
Make 56

2. For each basket base sew one 2½" Fabric A square to each unit from step 1 as shown. Make twenty-eight of each. Press.

2½
2½

Make 28 of each

3. Refer to Quick Corner Triangle directions on page 216. Using 4½" Fabric A and Fabric F squares, make twenty-eight units. Press.

A = 4½ x 4½
F = 4½ x 4½
Make 28

4. Sew one matching-colored unit from step 2 to bottom of unit from step 3. Press. Make a total of twenty-eight.

Make 28

5. Sew one 2½" Fabric A square to each remaining unit from step 2. Press. Make a total of twenty-eight.

2½

Make 28

6. Sew each unit from step 5 to matching-colored unit from step 4. Press. Block will measure 6½" square.

Make 28

7. From remaining scraps of Fabric F colors, cut seven 1" x 7" bias strips from each color. Fold each strip right sides together. Stitch along unfinished edge to make ¼" bias tube. Turn and press with ¼" bias bar. Make twenty-eight.

8. Position handles over matching-colored baskets with short raw edges overlapping seams as shown. Machine or hand stitch handles in place, opening seams as necessary to insert raw edges. Restitch seams. Press.

Open seam and insert raw edge

ASSEMBLY

1. Measure quilt through center from side to side. Trim two 1¼" x 42" second accent border strips to this measurement. Sew to top and bottom. Press seams toward accent border.

2. Measure quilt through center from top to bottom, including border. Trim remaining 1¼" x 42" second accent border strips to this measurement. Sew to sides. Press. At this point quilt will measure 24½" square.

3. Cut 18¼" squares in half once diagonally to make four outside setting triangles.

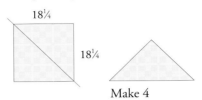

18¼

18¼

Make 4

4. Sew one corner triangle to each side of quilt. Press seams toward accent border.

5. Repeat steps 1 and 2 to fit, trim, and sew 1½"-wide border strips to top, bottom, and sides of quilt. Press seams toward border. Quilt will measure 36½" square.

6. Refer to project layout on page 22. Lay out a pleasing horizontal row of six small Basket Blocks and sew together. Press. Make a total of two rows.

7. Repeat step 6 to make two rows of eight small Basket Blocks. Press.

8. Sew rows from step 6 to opposite sides of quilt. Press seams toward accent strip. Sew rows from step 7 to remaining two sides. Press.

LAYERING AND FINISHING

1. Cut backing fabric crosswise into two equal pieces. Sew pieces together on the long edges to make one 54" x 84" (approximate) backing piece. Arrange and baste backing, batting, and top together referring to Layering the Quilt on page 217.

2. Hand or machine quilt as desired.

3. Cut one 2¾" x 42" binding strip into four equal pieces. Sew one piece to each remaining 2¾" x 42" strip. Refer to Binding the Quilt directions on page 217 to finish.

appliqué pattern pieces
Sunshine Basket Quilt

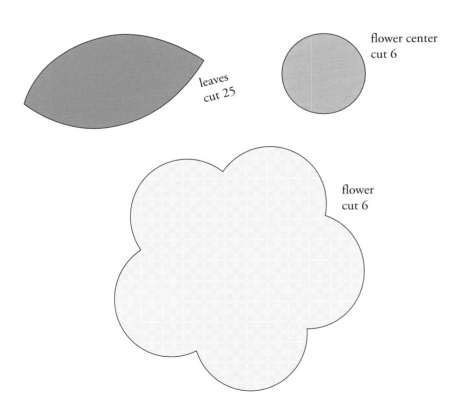

leaves
cut 25

flower center
cut 6

flower
cut 6

BASKET WEAVE QUILT

Finished Quilt Size: 91" x 100"

Photo: page 20

"HOW DID YOU DO THAT?"

That's the question your friends will ask as they admire the intricate basket weave design of this clever quilt. Only you will know how simple it was with its quick and efficient rotary-cut, strip-pieced construction. Read all instructions before beginning and use ¼"-wide seams throughout.

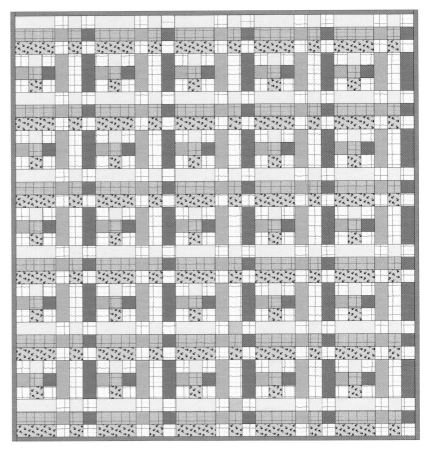

Quilt Layout

FABRIC REQUIREMENTS

Fabric A *(block 1 and block 3)*
  1⅜ yards

Fabric B *(block 1 and block 3)*
  1⅜ yards

Fabric C *(block 1 and block 3)*
  1⅜ yards

Fabric D *(block 2 and block 3)*
  1¼ yards

Fabric E *(block 2 and block 3)*
  2¾ yards

Fabric F *(block 2 and block 3)*
  1¼ yards

Backing - 8¼ yards

Binding - ⅞ yard

Lightweight batting
  99" x 108" piece

FABRIC KEY

Fabric A

Fabric B

Fabric C

Fabric D

Fabric E

Fabric F

CUTTING THE STRIPS AND PIECES

Read first paragraph of Cutting the Strips and Pieces on page 5.

Fabric A strips *(block 1 and block 3)*
* Thirteen 3½" x 42" strips

Fabric B *(block 1 and block 3)*
* Thirteen 3½" x 42" strips

Fabric C *(block 1 and block 3)*
* Thirteen 3½" x 42" strips

Fabric D *(block 2 and block 3)*
* Twelve 3½" x 42" strips

Fabric E *(block 2 and block 3)*
* Twenty-seven 3½" x 42" strips

Fabric F *(block 2 and block 3)*
* Twelve 3½" x 42" strips

Binding
* Ten 2¾" x 42" strips

MAKING THE BLOCKS

You will be making a total of one hundred ten blocks in three different block variations: thirty of block one, twenty-five of block two, and fifty-five of block three. All blocks will measure 9½" square.

Whenever possible, use the assembly line method for each step. Position pieces right sides together next to your sewing machine. Stitch first unit together, then continue sewing others without breaking threads. When all units are sewn, clip threads to separate them. Press in direction of arrows in diagrams.

BLOCK ONE

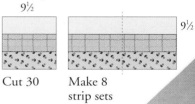

Sew one 3½" x 42" Fabric B strip between a 3½" x 42" Fabric A and Fabric C strip to make eight 9½" x 42" strip sets. Press. Using rotary cutter and ruler, cut thirty 9½" segments from strip sets. Label them Block One. Block will measure 9½" square.

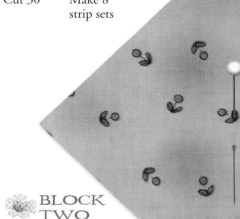

9½

Cut 30   Make 8
            strip sets

BLOCK TWO

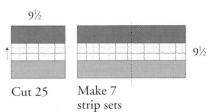

Sew one 3½" x 42" Fabric E strip between a 3½" x 42" Fabric D and Fabric F strip to make seven 9½" x 42" strip sets. Press. Using rotary cutter and ruler, cut twenty-five 9½" segments from strip sets. Label them Block Two.

9½

Cut 25   Make 7
            strip sets

BLOCK THREE

1. Sew one 3½" x 42" Fabric A strip between two 3½" x 42" Fabric E strips to make five 9½" x 42" strip sets. Press. Using rotary cutter and ruler, cut fifty-five 3½" segments from strip sets.

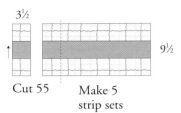

3½

9½

Cut 55   Make 5
strip sets

2. Sew one 3½" x 42" Fabric B strip between 3½" x 42" Fabric D and Fabric F strips to make five 9½" x 42" strip sets. Press. Using rotary cutter and ruler, cut fifty-five 3½" segments from strip sets.

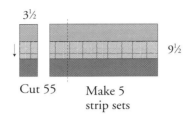

3½

9½

Cut 55   Make 5
strip sets

3. Sew one 3½" x 42" Fabric C strip between two 3½" x 42" Fabric E strips to make five 9½" x 42" strip sets. Press. Using rotary cutter and ruler, cut fifty-five 3½" segments from strip sets.

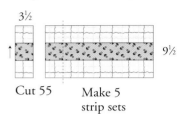

3½

9½

Cut 55   Make 5
strip sets

4. Sew one unit from step 2 between one unit from steps 1 and 3 as shown. Press. Make fifty-five. Label them Block Three. Block will measure 9½" square.

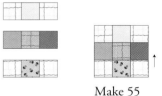

Make 55

❋ A white picket fence becomes a cheerful accent to your room with this Debbie Mumm® wallpaper and borders from Imperial Home Décor Group. Call (800) 539-5399 or visit www.imp-wall.com.

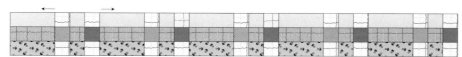

ASSEMBLY

1. Arrange five Block One and five Block Three to make a horizontal row, alternating the two block variations as shown. Press seams toward Block One. Make six rows and label them Row A.

Make 6 rows
Row A

2. Arrange five Block Three and five Block Two in a horizontal row, alternating the two block variations as shown. Press seams toward Block Two. Make five rows and label them Row B.

Make 5 rows
Row B

3. Referring to layout on page 30, lay out alternating A and B rows. Begin with an A row. Join rows and press.

LAYERING AND FINISHING

1. Cut backing fabric crosswise into three equal pieces. Sew pieces together on long edges to make one 99" x 126" (approximate) backing piece. Arrange and baste backing, batting, and top together referring to Layering the Quilt directions on page 217.

2. Hand or machine quilt as desired.

3. Sew eight 2 ¾" x 42" binding strips together in pairs. Cut two remaining strips in half and sew halves to each pieced strip. Refer to Binding the Quilt directions on page 217 to finish.

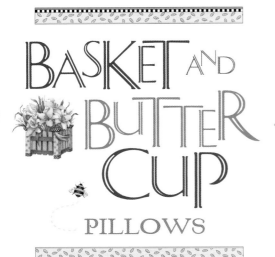

BASKET AND BUTTERCUP PILLOWS

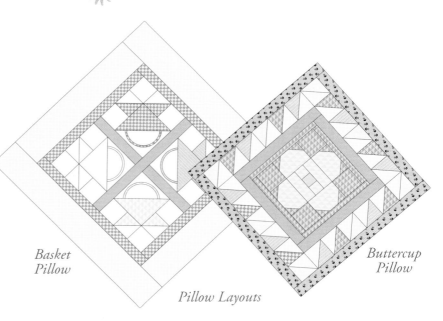

Basket Pillow

Pillow Layouts

Buttercup Pillow

Basket Pillow - 18" square

Buttercup Pillow - 16" square

Photo: page 20

THE PERFECT ACCENT TO OUR SUNSHINE

Basket Quilt, these cheery pillows are sure to brighten even the rainiest of mornings. Read all instructions before beginning and use ¼"-wide seams throughout.

FABRIC REQUIREMENTS

	Basket Pillow	Buttercup Pillow
Fabric A	⅙ yard each of four different fabrics *(baskets)*	¼ yard *(buttercup and border triangles)*
Fabric B	⅓ yard *(background)*	⅙ yard *(buttercup background and sashing)*
Fabric C		assorted scraps *(triangle border)*
Fabric D		assorted scraps *(triangle border)*
Sashing	⅛ yard	
Accent Border	⅛ yard *(accent)*	
Border	¼ yard	⅛ yard
Batting	22" square	20" square
Backing	½ yard	⅜ yard
Lining	22" square	20" square
Pillow Form	18"	16"

BASKET PILLOW

CUTTING THE STRIPS AND PIECES

Read first paragraph of Cutting the Strips and Pieces on page 5.

Fabric A *(baskets)*

* One 4½" square
* Two 2½" squares
* One 1" x 7" bias strip

Repeat for each of four fabrics.

Fabric B *(background)*

* One 4½" x 42" strip, cut into
  * Four 4½" squares
* Two 2½" x 42" strips, cut into
  * Twenty 2½" squares

Sashing

* One 1" x 42" strip, cut into
  * One 1" x 13" strip
  * Two 1" x 6½" strips

Accent Border

* Two 1" x 42" strips, cut into
  * Two 1" x 14" strips
  * Two 1" x 13" strips

Border

* Two 2¾" x 42" strips, cut into
  * Two 2¾" x 18½" strips
  * Two 2¾" x 14" strips

Backing

* One 12¾" x 42" strip, cut into
  * Two 12¾" x 18½" pieces

MAKING THE BLOCKS

BASKET BLOCKS

1. Refer to Small Basket Block directions on page 27. Repeat steps 1-8 for each of four Basket Blocks except-

* In step 1, make eight of each.
* In step 2, make four of each.
* In step 3, make four of each.
* In step 4, make four of each.
* In step 5, make four of each.
* In step 7, make four of each.

ASSEMBLY

1. Referring to project layout on page 34, arrange blocks to make two rows with two blocks each. Sew 1" x 6½" sashing strips between blocks. Press seams toward sashing strips. Sew 1" x 13" sashing strip between the two rows of blocks. Press.

2. Sew 1" x 13" accent border strips to top and bottom. Press seams toward accent border. Sew remaining accent border strips to sides. Press.

3. Sew 2¾" x 14" border strips to top and bottom and 2¾" x 18½" border strips to sides. Press seams toward border.

4. Layer batting between top and lining. Baste. Hand or machine quilt as desired. Trim batting and lining even with raw edge of pillow top.

LAYERING AND FINISHING

1. Narrow hem one long edge of each 12¾" x 18½" backing piece by folding under ¼" to wrong side. Press. Fold again ¼" to wrong side. Press. Topstitch along folded edge.

2. With right sides up, lay one backing piece over second piece so hemmed edges overlap, making single 18½" square backing panel. Baste pieces together at top and bottom where they overlap.

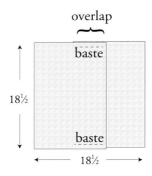

overlap

baste

18½

baste

18½

3. With right sides together, position and pin pillow top to backing. Using ¼" seam, sew around edges. Trim corners, turn right side out, and press.

4. Insert pillow form into pillow cover.

BUTTERCUP PILLOW

CUTTING THE STRIPS AND PIECES

Read first paragraph of Cutting the Strips and Pieces on page 5.

Fabric A

* Two 2½" x 42" strips, cut into
  • Four 2½" x 3½" pieces *(buttercup)*
  • Twenty-four 2½" squares *(border triangles)*
* One 1½" x 42" strip, cut into
  • Two 1½" x 3½" pieces *(buttercup)*
  • Two 1½" squares *(buttercup)*

Fabric B

* One 2½" x 14" strip, cut into
  • Four 2½" squares *(buttercup background)*
* One 1½" x 16" strip, cut into
  • Eight 1½" squares *(buttercup background)*
* One 1" x 42" strip, cut into
  • Two 1" x 8½" pieces *(sashing)*
  • Two 1" x 7½" pieces *(sashing)*

Fabric C

* One 1½" x 42" strip, cut into
  • One 1½" square *(buttercup center)*
  • Two 1½" x 10½" pieces *(accent border)*
  • Two 1½" x 8½" pieces *(accent border)*

Fabric D *(border triangles)*

* Twenty-four 2½" squares

Border

* Two 1½" x 42" strips, cut into
  • Two 1½" x 16½" strips
  • Two 1½" x 14½" strips

Backing

* One 11" x 42" strip, cut into
  • Two 11" x 16½" pieces

MAKING THE BLOCKS

BUTTERCUP BLOCK

1. Refer to Buttercup Block directions on page 12. Repeat steps 1-6 for one Buttercup Block except-

• In step 1, make one.

• In step 2, make one.

• In step 3, make four of each.

• In step 4, make two.

• In step 5, make one.

2. Sew 1" x 7½" sashing strips to top and bottom. Press seams toward sashing strips.

3. Sew 1" x 8½" sashing strips to sides. Press.

BORDERS

1. Sew 1½" x 8½" accent border strips to top and bottom. Press seams toward accent border. Sew 1½" x 10½" accent border strips to sides. Press.

2. Refer to Quick Corner Triangle directions on page 216. Using 2½" Fabric A and Fabric D squares, make twenty-four units. Press.

A = 2½ x 2½
D = 2½ x 2½
Make 24

3. Arrange five units from step 2 in a pleasing order. Sew together to make a strip. Press. Make four strips.

Make 4

4. Referring to project layout on page 34, sew a strip from step 3 each to top and bottom. Press seams toward accent border.

5. Sew one remaining unit from step 2 to each end of remaining strips from step 3 as shown. Sew to sides. Press.

6. Sew 1½" x 14½" border strips to top and bottom. Press seams toward border.

7. Sew 1½" x 16 ½" border strips to sides. Press.

8. Layer batting between top and lining. Baste. Hand or machine quilt as desired. Trim batting and lining even with raw edge of pillow top.

LAYERING AND FINISHING

1. Using two 11" x 16½" pieces for backing, refer to Layering and Finishing directions on page 36. Repeat steps 1-4, except, in step 2, overlap pieces making a single 16½" square backing panel.

GARDEN PARTY

HOW ABOUT A *garden party? A blooming garden or a patio filled with pots of fragrant flowers can be the most festive spot in your home. Try having a picnic or a tea party among the blooms!*

With all nature's colorful help, creating a perfect setting on your patio is easy. Add a table with your favorite tea set and Mother Nature will do the rest!

GARDEN VIGNETTE DINNERWARE

WELCOME SPRING

QUILT

Finished Size: 57" x 75"

Photo: page 42

SPRING IS ALWAYS RIGHT AROUND THE

corner when you snuggle under this colorful little quilt, the perfect size for a decadent afternoon nap! Flowerlike shades of green and lavender combine to create a springtime mood. Read all instructions before beginning and use ¼"-wide seams throughout.

Quilt Layout

FABRIC REQUIREMENTS

Fabric A *(diamonds)* - ⅞ yard each of two different fabrics

Fabric B *(triangles)* - 1 yard each of green fabric and lavender fabric

Fabric C *(rectangles)* - ⅓ yard each of two different fabrics

Fabric D *(center squares)* - ⅛ yard each of two different fabrics

Lattice - 1½ yards

Corner Squares - ¼ yard

Accent Border - ¼ yard

Border - 1 yard

Binding - ⅝ yard

Backing - 3⅝ yards

Lightweight batting 65" x 82" piece

CUTTING THE STRIPS AND PIECES

Read first paragraph of Cutting the Strips and Pieces on page 5.

Fabric A (diamonds)

* Seven 3½" x 42" strips, cut into
  * Seventy-two 3½" squares (block one)
* Six 3½" x 42" strips, cut into
  * Sixty-eight 3½" squares (block two)

Fabric B (triangles)

* Fifteen 2" x 42" strips, cut into
  * Two hundred eighty-eight 2" squares (block one)
* Fourteen 2" x 42" strips, cut into
  * Two hundred seventy-two 2" squares (block two)

Fabric C (rectangles)

* Seven 1½" x 42" strips, cut into
  * Seventy-two 1½" x 3½" pieces (block one)
* Six 1½" x 42" strips, cut into
  * Sixty-eight 1½" x 3½" pieces (block two)

Fabric D (center squares)

* One 1½" x 42" strip, cut into
  * Eighteen 1½" squares (block one)
* One 1½" x 42" strip, cut into
  * Seventeen 1½" squares (block two)

Lattice

* Seventeen 2½" x 42" strips, cut into
  * Eighty-two 2½" x 7½" pieces

Corner Squares

* Three 2½" x 42" strips, cut into
  * Forty-eight 2½" squares

Accent Border

* Six 1" x 42" strips

Border

* Seven 4½" x 42" strips

Binding

* Seven 2¾" x 42" strips

MAKING THE BLOCKS

You'll be making thirty-five blocks total: eighteen Block One (green triangles) and seventeen Block Two (lavender triangles).

Whenever possible, use the assembly line method for each step. Position pieces right sides together and line up next to sewing machine. Stitch first unit together, then continue sewing others without breaking threads. When all units are sewn, clip threads to separate them.

Press in the direction of the arrows in diagrams.

BLOCK ONE

1. Refer to Quick Corner Triangle directions on page 216. Sew four 2" Fabric B squares to each 3½" Fabric A square. Press. Make a total of seventy-two.

Step 1   Step 2

A = 3½ x 3½
B = 2 x 2
Make 72

2. Sew one 1½" x 3½" Fabric C piece between two units from step 1. Press. Make a total of thirty-six.

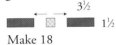

Make 36

3. Sew one 1½" Fabric D square between two matching 1½" x 3½" Fabric C pieces. Press. Make eighteen.

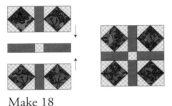

Make 18

4. Sew one unit from step 3 between two units from step 2. Press. Make eighteen. Block will measure 7½" square.

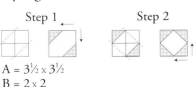

Make 18

 BLOCK TWO

1. Refer to Quick Corner Triangle directions on page 216. Sew four 2" Fabric B squares to each 3½" Fabric A square. Press. Make sixty-eight.

Step 1   Step 2

A = 3½ x 3½
B = 2 x 2
Make 68

2. Sew one 1½" x 3½" Fabric C piece between two units from step 1. Press. Make thirty-four.

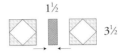

3. Sew one 1½" Fabric D square between two matching 1½" x 3½" Fabric C pieces. Press. Make seventeen.

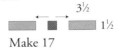

Make 17

4. Sew one unit from step 3 between two units from step 2. Press. Make seventeen. Block will measure 7½" square.

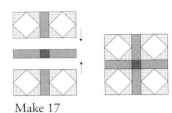

Make 17

 ASSEMBLY

1. Sew six 2½" corner squares and five 2½" x 7½" lattice pieces together in rows as shown. Repeat to make eight rows of lattice. Press.

Make 8

2. Refer to layout on page 42. Arrange blocks in seven horizontal rows with five blocks each, alternating Block One and Block Two in each row. Rows 1, 3, 5, and 7 begin with Block One, while Rows 2, 4, and 6 begin with Block Two.

3. For each row, sew 2½" x 7½" lattice pieces between blocks and to each end. Press seams toward lattice.

4. Sew lattice strips from step 1 to top and bottom and between rows of blocks. Press seams toward lattice.

 ADDING THE
BORDERS

1. Sew 1" accent border strips end to end to make one 1"-wide strip. Measure quilt through center from side to side. Cut two 1"-wide accent border strips to this measurement. Sew to top and bottom. Press seams toward accent borders.

2. Measure quilt through center from top to bottom, including borders. Cut two 1"-wide accent border strips to this measurement. Sew to sides. Press.

3. Sew 4½" x 42" border strips to make one continuous 4½"-wide strip. Repeat steps 1 and 2 to fit, trim, and sew 4½"-wide border strips to top, bottom, and sides of quilt. Press seams toward borders.

 LAYERING AND FINISHING

1. Cut backing fabric crosswise into two equal pieces. Sew pieces together on long edges to make one 65" x 84" (approximate) backing piece. Arrange and baste backing, batting, and top together, referring to Layering the Quilt directions on page 217.

2. Hand or machine quilt as desired.

3. Cut one 2¾" x 42" binding strip in half and sew halves to two 2¾" x 42" strips. Sew remaining 2¾" x 42" binding strips together in pairs. Using shorter strips for top and bottom and longer strips for sides, refer to Binding the Quilt directions on page 217 to finish.

 **WATERING CAN DINNERWARE**

Welcome spring to your table with this delightful dinnerware adorned with watering cans and festive flowers. For information on where to buy Debbie Mumm® dinnerware, visit www.debbiemumm.com or call (888) 819-2923.

HAND·PAINTED
WATERING
CAN

Checks, Stripes and Dots Watering Can

Photo: page 47

A WATERING CAN BE
USED FOR WATERING

your garden plants … or it can be used as a colorful accent on your patio or porch. With these quick and easy steps, you can transform a metal watering can into a piece of painted garden art.

MATERIALS NEEDED

Galvanized watering can

Household vinegar

Spray metal primer

Acrylic paints

Graphite paper

Paint brush

Toothbrush

Spray varnish

Daisy Watering Can

PREPARING THE WATERING CAN

1. Galvanized can needs to be washed with vinegar, rinsed well, and allowed to dry completely.

2. Spray watering can with a solid coat of spray metal primer. A light color is best.

PAINTING THE WATERING CAN

Apply base coat colors. This will generally require two coats for complete coverage.

ADDING DETAILS

Checks and stripes - On areas where checks or stripes are painted, apply lightest color first. Then paint stripes or checks over lighter base color.

Draw pattern on with a ruler and pencil to help keep lines straight. A checkerboard stencil can also be used to paint checks.

Dots - Dots on body of can are applied using the end of a paintbrush dipped in a contrasting color then dotted onto can. The larger the brush end, the larger the dot. Keep brush straight up and down and pick up fresh paint for every dot to create uniform shapes.

Daisy - Enlarge daisy template below to size that will fit can. Trace daisy onto piece of tracing paper. Using graphite paper between tracing paper and can, trace with pen over pattern onto can surface.

daisy template
enlarge to fit watering can

FINISHING TOUCHES

1. Paint all metal edges on can, spout, and handle with a contrasting color using small detail brush. Spray can with a matte finish varnish.

2. For an aged look apply an antiquing medium. Many products are available in water or oil base formulas. Follow manufacturer's instructions for best results.

3. A light splatter of dark acrylic paint will add to antique look. To apply, run thumb over a paint-filled toothbrush. Always test this on scrap paper first.

4. When dry, apply a finish coat of spray varnish. This comes in satin, matte, or gloss finishes.

POCKET FULL OF POSIES

GARDEN SHIRT

Photo: pages 38 and 39

A FAVORITE DENIM

SHIRT CAN BE

the beginning for this cute

and comfy gardening attire.

Pockets are deep and plentiful,

just right for holding gloves,

seed packets, and other

gardening necessities.

Make one as a gift for your

favorite gardener ... then

another, just for you!

Shirt Layout

MATERIALS AND FABRIC NEEDED

Border prints and other directional fabrics require additional yardage.

Fabric A *(deep pockets)* - 1⅛ yards

Fabric B *(deep pocket accent)* - ⅙ yard

Fabric C *(pocket flap, elbow patches, hankie)* - ⅜ yard

Fabric D *(back and shoulder accent strips)* - ⅙ yard

Assorted scraps - *(front shirt pocket, patches, label)*

Long-sleeve denim shirt

Buttons for front shirt pocket and to replace buttons on shirt front and cuffs

DEEP POCKETS WITH ACCENT TRIM

1. Measure around bottom edge of shirt from one inside edge of button placket to other inside edge of button placket. Add ½" to this measurement which will be Measurement A.

2. Cut two 18½" x 42" strips from Fabric A. Sew strips together end to end to make one 18½"-wide strip.

3. Trim strip from step 2 to Measurement A as determined in step 1. Strip now measures 18½" x Measurement A.

4. Fold strip in half lengthwise, right sides together. Using ¼ " seams, sew three raw (unfolded) edges, leaving an opening to turn. Clip corners, turn unit right side out, and press.

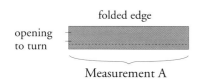

folded edge

opening to turn

Measurement A

5. Cut two 2" x 42" strips from Fabric B. Sew strips together end to end to make one 2"-wide strip.

6. Trim strip from step 5 to Measurement A as determined in step 1. Turn raw edge under ¼ " on all sides and press. Pin pressed strip even with top edge of pocket unit and topstitch in place.

7. Pin pocket unit from step 6 to shirt bottom, starting along inside edge of one button placket and ending along inside edge of opposite button placket. Attach with two rows of topstitching ¼" apart along side and bottom edges.

8. Space a series of vertical lines approximately 6" apart along pocket unit. Stitch two rows of stitching (¼" apart) along these lines to form pockets.

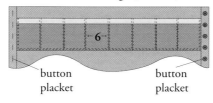

shirt bottom edge (laid flat)

6

button placket   button placket

PATCH POCKET WITH HANKIE

1. Cut two 6½" squares from scrap fabric. Pin squares right sides together. Using ¼" seams, sew all four sides leaving an opening to turn. Clip corners, turn unit right side out, and press.

6½

6½ leave open to turn

2. Refer to project illustration on page 48 to position and pin pocket to shirt front. Topstitch pocket in place along sides and bottom edge.

3. Cut one 12½" square from Fabric C. Hem all edges, fold, and tuck into pocket unit from step 2.

 DECORATIVE POCKET

1. Measure top edge of shirt's existing breast pocket and add ½" (Measurement B). Cut two pieces of Fabric C to measurements as shown.

Measurement B

2   2¾

2. Pin pieces right sides together. Using ¼" seams, sew all sides. Clip corners and make a small opening in one layer to allow for turning. Turn and press.

cut 1" opening

3. Pin flap to top edge of pocket and stitch in place. Secure point of flap with decorative button.

4. Cut one 3½" square from Fabric C. Turn raw edge under ¼" on all sides and press. Refer to project illustration to position patch on pocket. Stitch in place.

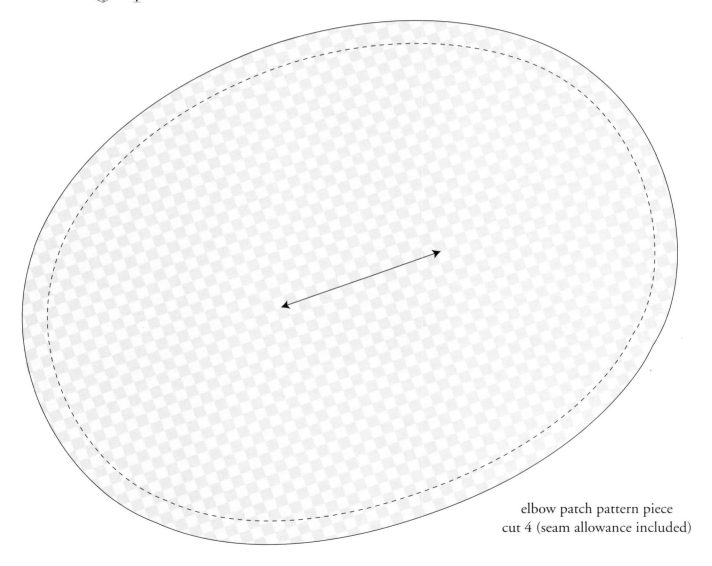

elbow patch pattern piece
cut 4 (seam allowance included)

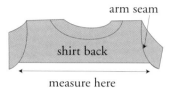
1. Refer to color photo on page 39. Cut one 4¼" x 42" Fabric D strip. Measure across shirt back along shoulder line from arm seam to arm seam. Add ½" to this measurement, which will be Measurement C.

arm seam

shirt back

measure here

2. Trim strip from step 1 to Measurement C. Strip now measures 4¼" x Measurement C. Turn raw edge under ¼" on all sides and press. Pin to shirt back and topstitch in place.

FINISHING TOUCHES

1. Replace buttons on denim shirt with buttons in your preferred colors.

2. Cut one 3¼" square from scrap. Turn raw edge under ¼" on all sides and press. Use this patch to create your own customized label, and stitch in place over manufacturer's label in shirt collar.

ELBOW PATCHES

1. Make elbow patch template from pattern on page 50. Cut four 8" x 6" pieces from Fabric C. For each patch, position two fabric pieces right sides together, trace around template, and cut on drawn line. Using ¼" seams, sew around entire raw edge. Clip curves and make a small opening in one layer to allow for turning. Turn and press.

2. Cut two 3¼" squares from scrap fabric. Turn raw edge under ¼" on all sides of each square and press. Position one square on each elbow patch. Stitch in place.

3. Refer to shirt layout on page 48. Position one elbow patch on each shirt sleeve and sew in place.

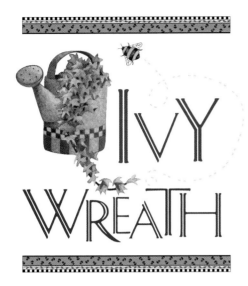

IVY WREATH

Wreath Layout

Photo: page 53

GARDEN ELEGANCE-
THAT'S WHAT YOU'LL
*create with this lovely wreath of
trailing ivy. Whether it graces your
front porch, your summer garden, or
your kitchen, it will add a truly
unique accent. Pots of fresh ivy
are added to a twig wreath to
wind in and out, and fanciful
garden ornaments give
it a colorful finishing touch.*

MATERIALS NEEDED

Twig wreath - 18" diameter

Three terra cotta pots - 3" planted
with ivy

Garden ornaments - Debbie
Mumm® Ornaments from
Creative Imaginations,
(800) 942-6487

Craft wire - 18 gauge

Glue gun and glue sticks

Raffia

FOR ANOTHER COUNTRY LOOK

*Make it a kitchen wreath!
Add planted pots of ivy to the
twig wreath, but for accents
use miniature kitchen
utensils and treasures, or
combine cookie cutters made
of copper or tin with vintage
measuring cups and spoons.
For inspiration visit your
favorite kitchen shop!*

TO CREATE YOUR WREATH

1. Begin by placing pots of ivy in a pleasing position at bottom of twig wreath. Secure in place using glue gun. Reinforce with wire and wind ends to back of wreath.

2. Wrap ivy vines around wreath, encircling it as much as possible with vines. Refer to color photo for reference. Tuck ends of vines into wreath.

3. For a finishing touch add small garden ornaments to ivy pots and wire garden ornaments to pots and sides of wreath. Make a raffia bow and wire to bottom of wreath, referring to photo below.

4. To give your ivy a good start in its new home, be sure and fertilize it generously with an all-purpose fertilizer for house plants.

FARMHOUSE KITCHEN

THE HEART OF THE

home ... the farmhouse kitchen radiates warmth and hospitality to everyone who stops by for a neighborly visit. There's always room for one more at the table when a delicious country breakfast of

farm-fresh eggs and hand-squeezed orange juice is served. So pull up a chair and help yourself to the irresistible fare and to the cozy warmth of this inviting country setting.

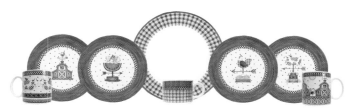

WEATHERVANE DINNERWARE

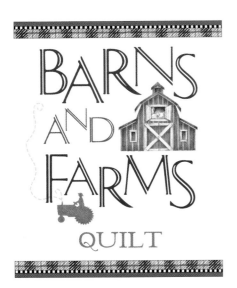

BARNS AND FARMS

QUILT

Finished Size: 63" x 71"

Photo: page 54

IMAGINE A PICTURE
PERFECT COUNTRY

*landscape, dotted with red barns,
neatly planted rows of crops, and
gaily whirling windmills ... then
bring this pleasant daydream home
with our charming Barns and Farms
quilt! Small appliqué accents add a
touch of realism to the quick-pieced
Barn Blocks, while three Windmill
Blocks are appliquéd in place to
highlight the traditional sashed set.
Read all instructions before beginning
and use ¼"-wide seams throughout.*

Quilt Layout

FABRIC REQUIREMENTS

Directional fabrics are not
recommended.

Fabric A *(barns)* - ¼ yard each of
four red fabrics

Fabric B *(sky)* - ⅝ yard

Fabric C *(four patches)* - ⅙ yard light
fabric

Fabric D *(four patches)* - ⅙ yard dark
fabric

Fabric E *(windmill blades)* - ⅙ yard

Fabric F *(windmill blades)* - ½ yard

Fabric G *(windmill background)*
⅓ yard

Crop Rows - ⅓ yard each of four
green fabrics

Frames and Timbers - ¼ yard

Doors - Four 4" x 4½" pieces

Windows - Four 2½" squares

Shutters - Eight 2½" x 1½" pieces

Roofs - Four 4½" x 8½" pieces

Sashing - 1⅓ yards

Accent Border - ⅓ yard

Border - ⅞ yard

Binding - ⅝ yard

Backing - 4 yards

Lightweight batting - 71" x 79"
piece

CUTTING THE STRIPS AND PIECES

Read first paragraph of Cutting the Strips and Pieces on page 5.

Fabric A (barns)

* One 4½" x 42" strip, cut into
  * One 4½" x 16½" piece
  * Two 4½" x 6" pieces
  * Two 2½" squares
* One 1½" x 20" strip, cut into
  * Two 1½" x 8½" pieces

Repeat for each of four fabrics.

Fabric B (sky)

* Four 4½" x 42" strips, cut into
  * Eight 4½" x 8½" pieces
  * Sixteen 4½" squares

Fabric C (four patches)

* Three 1½" x 42" strips

Fabric D (four patches)

* Three 1½" x 42" strips

Fabric E (windmill blades)

* One 4¼" x 42" strip, cut into
  * Nine 4¼" squares

Fabric F (windmill blades)

* Four 3⅛" x 42" strips

Fabric G (windmill background)

* One 4¼" x 42" strip, cut into
  * Nine 4¼" squares
* Four 1¼" x 42" strips

Crop Rows

* Five 2" x 42" strips

Repeat for each of four fabrics.

Frames and Timbers

* Two 1½" x 42" strips, cut into
  * Eight 1½" x 8" pieces (roof timbers)
* Four 1" x 42" strips, cut into
  * Four 1" x 8" pieces (roof timbers)
  * Eight 1" x 6" pieces (door timbers)
  * Twelve 1" x 4½" pieces (door frames)

Sashing

* Seventeen 2½" x 42" strips, cut into
  * Six 2½" x 34½" strips
  * Ten 2½" x 16½" strips
  * Thirty-six 2½" x 6½" pieces

Accent Border

* Seven 1" x 42" strips

Border

* Seven 4" x 42" strips

Binding

* Seven 2¾" x 42" strips

MAKING THE BLOCKS

You'll be making four Barn Blocks that will measure 16½" and nine sashed Windmill Blocks that will measure 10½".

Whenever possible, use the assembly line method for each step. Position pieces right sides together and line up next to your sewing machine. Stitch first unit together, then continue sewing others without breaking threads. When all units are sewn, clip threads to separate them. Press in direction of arrows in diagrams.

 ## BARN BLOCKS

1. Machine stitch or refer to Hand Appliqué directions on page 216. Appliqué two 1" x 6" door timber pieces to form an "x" over each 4½" x 4"door piece as shown. Trim edges of appliquéd pieces even with edges of fabric. Make a total of four.

Make 4

2. Sew one 1" x 4½" door frame piece to top edge of each unit from step 1.

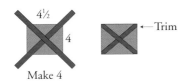

Make 4

3. Arrange and sew one unit from step 2, two 1" x 4½" door frame pieces, and two matching 4½" x 6" Fabric A pieces as shown. Press. Make a total of four.

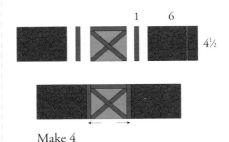

Make 4

4. Refer to Quick Corner Triangle directions on page 216. Sew two 4½" Fabric B squares to each 4½" x 16½" Fabric A piece. Press. Make a total of four.

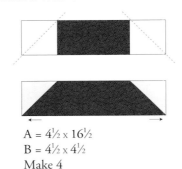

A = 4½ x 16½
B = 4½ x 4½
Make 4

5. Sew units from step 3 to matching units from step 4 in pairs as shown. Press. Make four.

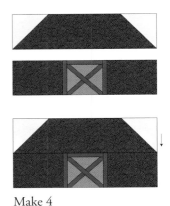

Make 4

6. Arrange and sew two matching 2½" Fabric A squares, two 2½" x 1½" shutter pieces, and one 2½" window square as shown. Press. Make a total of four.

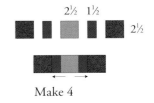

Make 4

7. Sew each unit from step 6 between two matching 1½" x 8½" Fabric A pieces. Press. Make four.

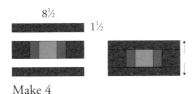

Make 4

8. Refer to Quick Corner Triangle directions on page 216. Sew two remaining 4½" Fabric B squares to each 4½" x 8½" roof piece. Press. Make a total of four.

Roof = 4½ x 8½
B = 4½ x 4½
Make 4

9. Sew units from step 7 to units from step 8 in pairs as shown. Press. Make four.

Make 4

10. Sew each unit from step 9 between two 4½" x 8½" Fabric B pieces. Press. Make a total of four.

4½

8½

Make 4

11. Sew units from step 5 to matching units from step 10 in pairs as shown. Press. Block will measure 16½" square.

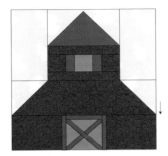

Make 4

12. Refer to project layout on page 58. Machine stitch or refer to Hand Appliqué directions on page 216. Appliqué one 1" x 8" timber piece at base and two 1½" x 8" timber pieces over peak of each roof.

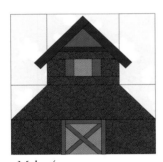

Make 4

FOUR PATCH BLOCKS

1. Sew 1½" x 42" Fabric C and 1½" x 42" Fabric D strips in pairs to make three strip sets measuring 2½" x 42". Press seams toward darker fabrics. Using rotary cutter and ruler, cut a total of seventy-two 1½" segments from strip sets.

1½

2½

Cut 72   Make 3
                strip sets

2. Sew segments from step 1 in pairs as shown. Make thirty-six units. Press.

Make 36

 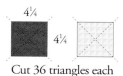

WINDMILL BLOCKS

1. Cut each 4¼" Fabric E square in half twice diagonally to make thirty-six triangles. Repeat, using 4¼" Fabric G squares.

Cut 36 triangles each

2. Sew Fabric E and G triangles from step 1 in pairs along one short side to make thirty-six two-triangle units as shown. Press.

Make 36

3. Sew 3⅛" x 42" Fabric F and 1¼" x 42" Fabric G strips in pairs to make four strip sets. Press. Using rotary cutter and ruler, cut a total of thirty-six 3⅞" segments from the strip sets.

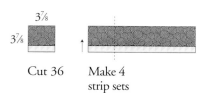

Cut 36   Make 4
          strip sets

4. Cut each 3⅞" segment from step 3 in half once diagonally to make two triangles. The triangles labeled * will be used to complete the blocks.

 *Use this triangle

5. Sew triangle units from step 2 to triangle units from step 4 in pairs along their long edges. Press. Make a total of thirty-six.

Make 36

6. Sew units from step 5 together in pairs as shown. Press. Make a total of eighteen.

Make 18

7. Sew units from step 6 together in pairs as shown. Press. Make nine.

Make 9

Nostalgia is remembering the pleasures of our old kitchen when we were kids, without remembering how long it took to wash the dishes.

Caroline Brownlow

from the book
Tea Time Friends
Brownlow©1999
illustrated by Debbie Mumm®

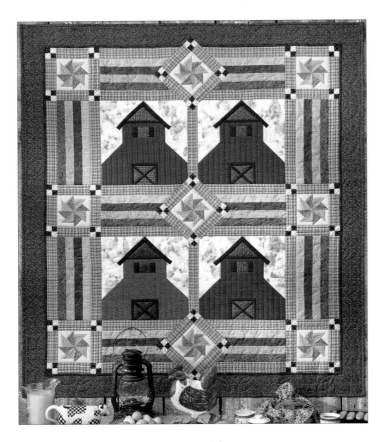

CROP ROWS

1. Sew one each of four different 2" x 42" green strips together to make a strip set measuring 6½" x 42". Press. Make five strip sets. Using rotary cutter and ruler, cut one 34½" segment from each of three strip sets, and two 16½" segments from each of two remaining strip sets.

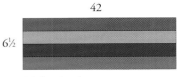

Make 5 strip sets

2. Sew each 6½" x 34½" segment from step 1 between two 2½" x 34½" sashing strips. Press seams toward sashing strips. Make three. Repeat to sew each 6½" x 16½" segment from step 1 between two 2½" x 16½" sashing strips. Press. Make four.

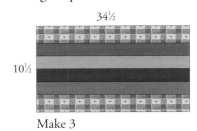

Make 3

Make 4

8. Sew each Windmill unit from step 7 between two 2½" x 6½" sashing strips. Press. Make a total of nine.

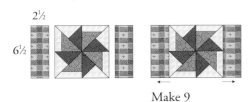

Make 9

9. Sew each remaining 2½" x 6½" sashing strip between two four-patch blocks as shown. Press. Make eighteen.

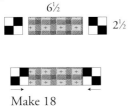

Make 18

10. Sew each unit from step 8 between two units from step 9. Press. Make nine. Block will measure 10½" square.

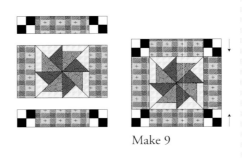

Make 9

=Baaa

1. Arrange two Barn Blocks, two 16½" sashed Crop Rows, and one 2½" x 16½" sashing strip in a horizontal row as shown. Sew the blocks, sashed rows, and sashing strip together. Press seams away from Barn Blocks. Make two rows.

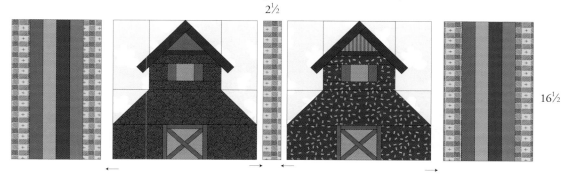

2½

16½

Make 2 rows

2. Sew each 34½" sashed Crop Row between two Windmill Blocks as shown. Press seams away from Windmill Blocks. Make three rows.

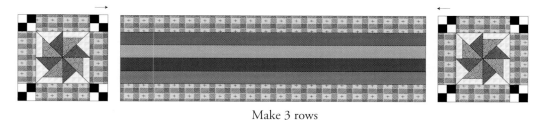

Make 3 rows

3. Referring to project layout on page 56, arrange rows in their proper order. Join rows and press.

4. Cut one 1" x 42" accent border strip in half and sew halves to two accent border strips. Measure quilt through center from side to side. Trim strips to this measurement. Sew to top and bottom. Press toward accent border.

5. Sew remaining accent border strips together in pairs. Measure quilt through center from top to bottom. Trim strips to this measurement. Sew to sides. Press.

6. Repeat steps 4 and 5 for measuring and add 4" borders to quilt in same manner.

7. Machine stitch or refer to Hand Appliqué directions on page 216. Turn each remaining Windmill Block on point and appliqué in place as shown in the project layout on page 56.

Cock-a-doodle-do!

LAYERING AND FINISHING

1. Cut backing fabric crosswise into two equal pieces. Sew pieces together on long edges to make one 72" x 84" (approximate) backing piece. Arrange and baste backing, batting, and top together, referring to Layering the Quilt directions on page 217.

2. Machine or hand quilt as desired.

3. Cut one 2¾" x 42" binding strip in half and sew halves to two 2¾" x 42" strips. Sew remaining 2¾" x 42" binding strips together in pairs. Using shorter strips for top and bottom and longer strips for sides, refer to Binding the Quilt directions on page 217 to finish.

Good Mornin'!

© Debbie Mumm

WEATHERVANE DINNERWARE

Deep shades of barn red and warm gold set the tone for this delightful collection of Americana barns and farm designs. Truly a unique dinnerware collection! For information on where to buy Debbie Mumm® dinnerware, visit www.debbiemumm.com or call (888) 819-2923.

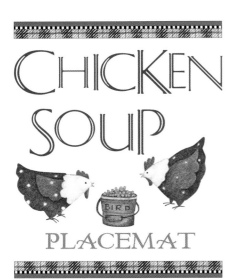

CHICKEN SOUP

PLACEMAT

Finished Size: 14½" square

Photo: page 55

WHETHER IT'S BREAKFAST, LUNCH, OR

dinner, this charming chicken adds rustic charm to any mealtime. Ours is hand appliquéd, but you can substitute the quick-fuse method if you prefer. Fabric requirements and cutting instructions are for a single placemat; make as many as you need for your country table. Read all instructions before beginning and use ¼"-wide seams throughout.

Placemat Layout

FABRIC REQUIREMENTS

ONE PLACEMAT:

Background - 8½" square

Appliqués - Assorted scraps for feet, body, wing, face, comb

Inside Border - ⅛ yard

Middle Border - ⅛ yard

Outside Border - ⅙ yard

Backing - 15" square

Low-loft batting - 15" square

Embroidery floss

CUTTING THE STRIPS AND PIECES

Read first paragraph of Cutting the Strips and Pieces on page 5.

Inside Border

❋ One 1½" x 42" strip, cut into
- Two 1½" x 8½" strips
- Two 1½" x 10½" strips

Middle Border

❋ Two 1" x 42" strips, cut into
- Two 1" x 10½" strips
- Two 1" x 11½" strips

Outside Border

❋ Two 2¼" x 42" strips, cut into
- Two 2¼" x 11½" strips
- Two 2¼" x 15" strips

PREPARING FOR APPLIQUÉ

1. Trace appliqué designs from page 68. Make templates and use assorted scraps to trace one each of pieces 1 (feet), 2 (body), 3 (wing), 4 (comb), 5 (head), and 6 (face and eye). Cut out appliqués, adding ¼" seam allowance around each piece.

2. Fold 8½" background block in half on both diagonals and press lightly to find centerpoint. Referring to placement diagram on page 66, turn block on point and position appliqués. Use preferred method to stitch appliqués in place.

3. Referring to pattern on page 68 for placement, use two strands of embroidery floss to make French knot eye and three strands of floss to embroider beak. Refer to Embroidery Stitch Guide on page 216.

BORDERS

Sew short inside border strips to two opposite sides of block. Press seams away from block. Sew long inside border strips to two remaining sides of block. Press. Repeat to add middle and then outside borders to all four sides of block. Press.

LAYERING AND FINISHING

1. Position top and backing right sides together. Center both pieces on top of batting and pin all three layers together. Using ¼" seams, sew around edges, leaving an opening for turning.

2. Trim backing and batting to same size as top. Trim corners, turn right side out, hand stitch opening closed, and press.

3. Machine or hand quilt as desired.

appliqué pattern pieces
Chicken Soup Placemat

MAKE IT A
WALLHANGING

Our Chicken Soup Placemat will bring a whimsical touch to your kitchen table, but that's not the only spot you can use it.

How about on your kitchen wall? Our fun and friendly chicken can be the perfect accent to your décor when you create it in colors that coordinate with your kitchen.

We've created ours in rich tones of black and red, but it will have an entirely different personality when you make it from bright, bold tones … or even from an assortment of your favorite scraps. Any way you make it, Chicken Soup is always "just what the doctor ordered!"

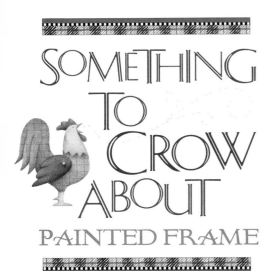

SOMETHING TO CROW ABOUT
PAINTED FRAME

Photo: page 71

Frame Layout

YOU'LL REALLY HAVE "SOMETHING TO CROW

about" when you create this lovely country-style wooden frame to showcase a favorite print. With our careful step-by-step instructions, you can easily paint this unique accent in colors that will highlight your own home décor.

MATERIALS NEEDED

Frame - unfinished wood

Liner brush and #2 flat brush

Sponge brush

Tracing paper and graphite paper

Graphite pencil or white chalk pencil

Scotch™ Magic™ Tape *(no substitution recommended)*

Antiquing medium

Matte craft varnish

Acrylic paints - red, gold, green, black, ivory, tan

Sandpaper

Debbie Mumm® "A Little Something to Crow About" - print from Wild Apple Graphics, (800) 756-8359 (no longer available)

PAINTING THE FRAME

1. Paint flat surface of frame with a thin wash of red paint. Allow it to dry completely for several hours or overnight.

2. Sand lightly to smooth surface.

3. Draw a line ⅛" around frame opening using a graphite or white chalk pencil.

4. Place tape on outside edge of pencil line. Press firmly.

5. Using edge of tape as a stencil line, paint the strip along inside edge with ivory.

6. With a ruler and the tape still in place, measure and draw ⅛" checks using a pencil to mark border.

7. Paint every other check black. Sand lightly to give an antiqued look. Remove tape.

8. Measure and draw a guideline ⅜" from outside edge of frame. Apply tape along inside of drawn edge. Press firmly.

9. Paint along edge with tan. Leave tape in place and lightly sponge with ivory over tan to give a mottled look. Remove tape.

10. Trace pattern for vine and corner pieces onto a piece of tracing paper. Using graphite paper between tracing paper and wood, trace with a pen over pattern onto wood surface. Do this for vine and corner pieces.

11. Using liner brush and dark green paint slightly thinned, paint vine and leaf pattern. Let dry. To give an antiqued look, lightly sand.

12. Using diagram as a guide, paint corner pieces with gold, green, red, and tan.

13. Paint outside edge of frame green. Paint inside edge of frame red.

14. Spray lightly with a matte craft varnish. Antique following directions on a purchased antiquing medium.

15. When dry spray again with a matte varnish.

MORE OPTIONS:

A very simple frame could be achieved by using different techniques such as sponging, crackling, or simple staining. Any of these techniques combined with a simple checked border will help you create a delightful frame for any favorite print.

•

It's easy to create a fabric-covered mat to match your print. First, cut a piece of mat board and fabric slightly larger than the finished size of the mat. Apply fusible web to the wrong side of the fabric according to manufacturer's instructions. Remove the paper and iron onto the mat board. Be sure the fabric is adhered well to the mat board, then cut the mat to the desired size.

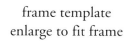

frame template
enlarge to fit frame

COUNTRY VINTAGE KITCHEN

WARM, FRESHLY baked bread ... close your eyes and you can almost smell its irresistible aroma when you step into this country vintage kitchen. This charming setting with its quilts of red, blue, and yellow brings back wonderful memories of sitting around the stove at grandma's house. For just a short while, slow down life's busy pace and enjoy a nostalgic visit to yesterday.

COUNTRY VINTAGE KITCHEN DINNERWARE

73

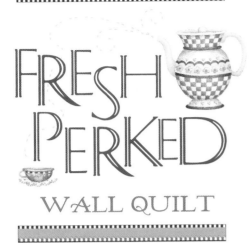

FRESH PERKED
WALL QUILT

Finished Size: 39" square

Photo: page 72

M·M·M·M! JAVA JOE, CAFE-
YOU'LL ALMOST SMELL

the coffee beans roasting as you stitch
this delightful tribute to
America's favorite morning brew!
Quick-pieced construction leaves you
time to spare – perfect for settling
in with your favorite mug, a
tasty treat, and that new quilting
book you've longed to browse.
Read all instructions before
beginning and use ¼"-wide
seams throughout.

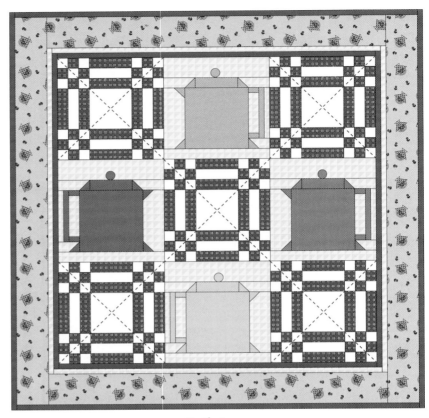

Quilt Layout

FABRIC REQUIREMENTS

Directional fabrics are
not recommended.

Fabric A *(coffee pots)* - ¼ yard each
  of four fabrics

Fabric B *(background)* - ½ yard

Fabric C *(checkerboard blocks)*
  ½ yard of dark fabric

Fabric D *(checkerboard blocks)*
  ⅝ yard of light fabric

First Accent Border - ⅙ yard

Second Accent Border - ⅙ yard

Border - ½ yard

Backing - 1¼ yards

Binding - ⅜ yard

Lightweight batting - 43" square

Buttons - Four ⅞"

Embroidery floss

CUTTING THE STRIPS AND PIECES

Read first paragraph of Cutting the Strips and Pieces on page 5.

Fabric A (coffee pots)

* One 6½" square
* One 1½" x 14" strip, cut into
  * One 1½" x 4½" piece
  * Five 1½" squares
* One 1" x 10" strip, cut into
  * One 1" x 5½" piece
  * Two 1" x 1½" pieces

Repeat for each of four fabrics.

Fabric B (background)

* Two 2½" x 42" strips, cut into
  * Four 2½" x 10½" pieces
  * Four 2½" x 6½" pieces
* Three 1½" x 42" strips, cut into
  * Four 1½" x 10½" pieces
  * Four 1½" x 4½" pieces
  * Eight 1½" x 3½" pieces
  * Four 1½" x 2½" pieces
* One 1" x 24" strip, cut into
  * Four 1" x 5½" pieces

Fabric C (checkerboard blocks)

* Ten 1½" x 42" strips

Fabric D (checkerboard blocks)

* One 4½" x 42" strip, cut into
  * Five 4½" squares
* Eight 1½" x 42" strips

First Accent Border

* Four 1" x 42" strips

Second Accent Border

* Four 1" x 42" strips

Border

* Four 3½" x 42" strips

Binding

* Five 2¾" x 42" strips

MAKING THE BLOCKS

You'll be making four Coffee Pot Blocks and five Checkerboard Blocks.

COFFEE POT BLOCKS

For all blocks, refer to Quick Corner Triangle directions on page 216.

1. Sew two 1½" Fabric A squares to each 2½" x 6½" Fabric B piece as shown. Press. Make a total of four.

A = 1½ x 1½
B = 2½ x 6½
Make 4

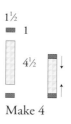

2. Sew one 1½" x 4½" Fabric B piece between two 1" x 1½" Fabric A pieces. Press. Make a total of four.

1½
1
4½
Make 4

3. Sew one 1" x 5½" Fabric A piece between one unit from step 2 and one 1" x 5½" Fabric B piece. Press. Make a total of four.

1
5½
Make 4

4. Sew a 1½" Fabric A square to short left side of a 1½" x 2½" Fabric B piece. Press. Make two. Repeat to sew a 1½" Fabric A square to short right side of remaining 1½" x 2½" Fabric B pieces. Press. Make two.

A = 1½ x 1½
B = 1½ x 2½
Make 2 of each

5. Sew one unit from step 4 to bottom edge of each unit from step 3. Be sure step 3 units are positioned as shown. Press. Make two of each.

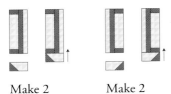

Make 2   Make 2

6. Sew one 6½" Fabric A square between one unit from step 1 and one unit from step 5. Be sure step 1 and step 5 units are positioned as shown. Press. Make two of each.

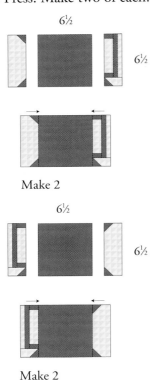

6½

6½

Make 2

6½

6½

Make 2

7. Sew a 1½" Fabric A square to the short right side of a 1½" x 3½" Fabric B piece. Press. Make four. Repeat to sew a 1½" Fabric A square to the short left side of remaining 1½" x 3½" Fabric B pieces. Press. Make a total of four.

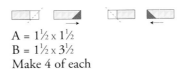

A = 1½ x 1½
B = 1½ x 3½
Make 4 of each

8. Sew one 1½" x 4½" Fabric A piece between two opposite units from step 7 as shown. Press. Make a total of four.

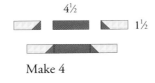

4½

1½

Make 4

9. Sew one 2½" x 10½" Fabric B piece, one unit from step 8, one unit from step 6, and one 1½" x 10½" Fabric B strip in order as shown. Press. Make two of each. Block will measure 10½" square.

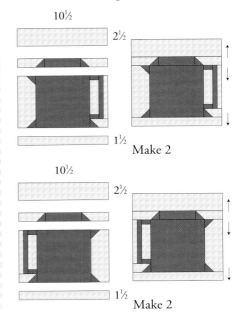

10½   2½

1½   Make 2

10½   2½

1½   Make 2

CHECKERBOARD BLOCKS

1. Sew one 1½" x 42" Fabric C strip between two 1½" x 42" Fabric D strips to make a strip set that measures 3½" x 42". Press. Make two strip sets. Using rotary cutter and ruler, cut forty 1½" segments from strip sets.

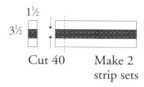

Cut 40   Make 2 strip sets

2. Sew one 1½" x 42" Fabric D strip between two 1½" x 42" Fabric C strips to make a strip set that measures 3½" x 42". Press. Make four strip sets. Using rotary cutter and ruler, cut twenty 1½" segments from one strip set.

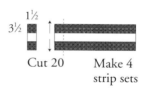

Cut 20   Make 4 strip sets

3. Sew one segment from step 2 between two segments from step 1 as shown. Press. Make twenty.

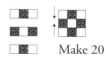

Make 20

4. Using rotary cutter and ruler, cut twenty 4½" segments from remaining strip sets from step 2.

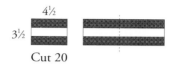

Cut 20

5. Sew one segment from step 4 between two units from step 3 as shown. Press. Make a total of ten.

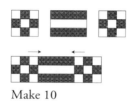

Make 10

6. Sew each 4½" Fabric D square between two segments from step 4. Press. Make a total of five.

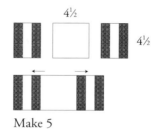

Make 5

7. Sew one unit from step 6 between two units from step 5. Press. Make a total of five. Block will measure 10½" square.

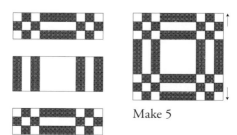

Make 5

USE YOUR VINTAGE LINENS

Maybe they're tucked away in a cupboard drawer or in an old attic trunk. Wherever you've stashed them, bring out those vintage napkins and use them! These treasures are much too lovely to be hidden away.

They add a delightful accent to a kitchen shelf when a corner is draped over the edge. Use them just as they are or sew on a bright fabric border to match your dinnerware and add your own hand embroidery.

To embroider the vintage-looking coffee pot seen in the photo on page 79, use the template on page 93 for an embroidery guide.

ASSEMBLY

1. Referring to project layout on page 74, arrange blocks into three horizontal rows of three alternating blocks. Rows 1 and 3 begin with Checkerboard Blocks. Row 2 begins with a Coffee Pot Block. Sew blocks into rows. Press seams toward Checkerboard Blocks.

2. Sew rows together. Press.

3. Measure quilt through center from side to side. Trim two 1" x 42" first accent border strips to this measurement. Sew to top and bottom. Press seams toward accent border.

4. Measure quilt through center from top to bottom, including border. Trim strips to this measurement. Sew to sides. Press.

5. Measure, trim, and add 1" second accent borders, and then 3½" borders in same manner.

LAYERING AND FINISHING

1. Arrange and baste backing, batting, and top together, referring to Layering the Quilt directions on page 217.

2. Machine or hand quilt as desired.

3. Cut one 2¾" x 42" binding strip in half and sew halves to two 2¾" x 42" strips. Using shorter strips for top and bottom and longer (pieced) strips for sides, refer to Binding the Quilt directions on page 217 to finish.

4. Refer to project layout and Embroidery Stitch Guide on page 216. Embroider running stitch through center of each block. Sew buttons to coffee pot lids.

COUNTRY VINTAGE
KITCHEN DINNERWARE

Tiny red and white checks border the charming kitchen images from yesterday in this nostalgic dinnerware. For information on where to buy Debbie Mumm® dinnerware, visit www.debbiemumm.com or call (888) 819-2923.

CHECKER BOARD CHURN DASH

TABLE QUILT

Finished Size: 50" square

Photo: page 83

WHETHER YOU LIVE IN A 100-YEAR-OLD

farmhouse or a sleek city condo, this updated version of the cozy Churn Dash pattern will feel right at home. High-contrast fabrics add punch to the crisp checkerboard bars, cut and pieced effortlessly from efficient strip-sets. You'll love our all-in-one method for adding mitered borders! Read all instructions before beginning and use ¼"-wide seams throughout.

Quilt Layout

FABRIC REQUIREMENTS

Fabric A *(corner triangles)* - ¼ yard each of four yellow fabrics

Fabric B *(background)* - ½ yard each of four blue fabrics

Fabric C *(checkerboard)* - ½ yard light fabric

Fabric D *(checkerboard)* - ½ yard red fabric

Accent Border - ¼ yard

Middle Border - ¼ yard

Outside Border - ⅝ yard

Binding - ½ yard

Backing - 3 yards

Lightweight batting - 54" square

CUTTING THE STRIPS AND PIECES

Read first paragraph of Cutting the Strips and Pieces on page 5.

Fabric A *(corner triangles)*

* Two 3½" x 42" strips, cut into
  • Sixteen 3½" squares

Repeat for each of four fabrics.

Fabric B *(background)*

* One 4½" x 42" strip, cut into
  • Four 4½" squares
* Two 3½" x 42" strips, cut into
  • Sixteen 3½" squares
* Two 1½" x 42" strips, cut into
  • Sixteen 1½" x 4½" pieces

Repeat for each of four fabrics.

Fabric C *(checkerboard)*

* Ten 1½" x 42" strips

Fabric D *(checkerboard)*

* Ten 1½" x 42" strips

Accent Border

* Five 1" x 42" strips

Middle Border

* Five 1½" x 42" strips

Outside Border

* Five 3½" x 42" strips

Binding

* Six 2¾" x 42" strips

MAKING THE BLOCKS

You will be making sixteen Checkerboard Churn Dash Blocks.

Whenever possible, use the assembly line method for each step. Position pieces right sides together and line up next to your sewing machine. Stitch first unit together, then continue sewing others without breaking threads. When all units are sewn, clip threads to separate them. Press in direction of arrows in diagrams.

CHECKERBOARD CHURN DASH BLOCKS

1. Alternate fabrics and sew two 1½" x 42" Fabric C and two 1½" x 42" Fabric D strips together to make a strip set that measures 4½" x 42". Press seams toward darker fabrics. Make five strip sets. Using rotary cutter and ruler, cut one hundred twenty-eight 1½" segments from strip sets.

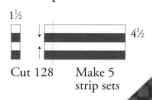

1½

4½

Cut 128   Make 5 strip sets

2. Sew one 1½" x 4½" Fabric B piece and two units from step 1 as shown. Press. Make sixty-four units.

4½

1½

Make 64

3. Refer to Quick Corner Triangle directions on page 216. Using 3½" Fabric A and B squares, make sixty-four units. Press.

A = 3½ x 3½
B = 3½ x 3½
Make 64

4. Sew one unit from step 2 between two matching units from step 3. Press. Make thirty-two.

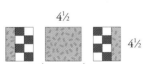

Make 32

5. Sew one 4½" Fabric B square between two matching units from step 2. Press. Make sixteen.

4½

4½

Make 16

6. Sew one unit from step 5 between two matching units from step 4 as shown. Press. Make sixteen. Block will measure 10½" square.

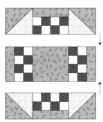

Make 16

ASSEMBLY

1. Arrange blocks in a pleasing arrangement of four horizontal rows with four blocks each. Sew blocks into rows. Press seams in opposite directions from row to row.

2. Sew rows together. Press.

MAKING AND ADDING THE MITERED BORDERS

1. Cut one 1" x 42" accent border strip into four equal pieces. Sew one piece to each remaining 1" x 42" accent border strip. Repeat to cut and piece 1½" middle border strips and 3½" outside border strips.

2. Sew one 1½" middle border strip between one 1" accent border strip and one 3½" outside border strip. Make four identical border units.

3. Measure quilt vertically and horizontally. Measurements should be the same. If they differ slightly, determine their average.

4. Fold each border unit crosswise to find its midpoint and mark with a pin. Using quilt dimension measured in step 3, measure each border unit from its midpoint and pin-mark border ends to show where edges of quilt will be.

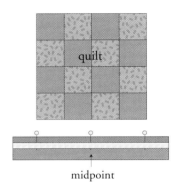

midpoint

5. Beginning at a marked end point, draw a 45 degree diagonal line to represent mitered seam line. Repeat on opposite end of strip, drawing a mirror-image diagonal line. Repeat for all four border units.

45°

6. Align a border unit to quilt with 1" inside border closest to quilt center. Pin at midpoints and pin-marked ends first, and then along entire side easing if necessary to fit.

7. Sew border to quilt, stopping and starting with a backstitch ¼" from pin-marked end points. Do not sew past pin marks at either end. Repeat to sew all four border units to quilt.

quilt front

8. Fold one corner diagonally, right sides together, matching and pinning marked diagonal sewing lines. End points of adjacent seams should match. Begin sewing with a backstitch at point where side seams ended. Sew to end of marked line at outside edge of strip. Trim excess border ¼" from seam and press open. Repeat on remaining corners.

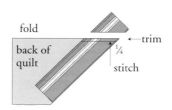

fold

back of quilt

trim

¼

stitch

LAYERING AND FINISHING

1. Cut backing fabric crosswise into two equal pieces. Sew pieces together on the long edges to make one 54" x 84" (approximate) backing piece. Arrange and baste backing, batting, and top together, referring to Layering the Quilt directions on page 217.

2. Hand or machine quilt as desired.

3. Cut two 2¾" x 42" binding strips in half. Sew one piece to each remaining 2¾" x 42" binding strip. Refer to Binding the Quilt directions on page 217 to finish.

VINTAGE COUNTRY

TABLE RUNNER

Finished Size: 17" x 42½"

Photo: page 85

SET THE PERFECT
COUNTRY TABLE

with this checkerboard of patchwork and embroidery. No need to fret over the unusual shape – a simple pillow-turn technique makes finishing a snap! Read all instructions before beginning and use ¼"-wide seams throughout.

Quilt Layout

FABRIC REQUIREMENTS

Fabric A *(block 1)* - One 2" x 6" strip of ten different fabrics

Fabric B *(block 1)* - ¼ yard red fabric and ⅛ yard yellow fabric

Fabric C *(block 2)* - ⅛ yard light fabric

Fabric D *(block 2)* - ¼ yard each of green and blue fabric

Backing - (minimum 44"-wide) ⅝ yard

Flannel or lightweight batting 19" x 44" piece

Embroidery floss - Assorted colors

CUTTING THE STRIPS AND PIECES

Read first paragraph of Cutting the Strips and Pieces on page 5.

Fabric B *(block 1)*

⁕ Two 2" x 42" strips, cut into
  • Six 2" x 6½" pieces (red)
  • Six 2" x 3½" pieces (red)

⁕ One 2" x 42" strip, cut into
  • Four 2" x 6½" pieces (yellow)
  • Four 2" x 3½" pieces (yellow)

Fabric C

❋ One 3½" x 42" strip, cut into

- Eight 3½" squares

Fabric D *(block 2)*

❋ Three 2" x 42" strips, cut into

- Eight 2" x 6½" pieces (green)
- Eight 2" x 3½" pieces (green)

Repeat for blue fabric.

MAKING THE BLOCKS

You will be making thirteen "framed" blocks: five Block One and eight Block Two. Block One is a scrappy four-patch surrounded by a red or yellow "frame." Block Two is a single, light-colored center square embellished with embroidery floss and surrounded by a green or blue frame.

 **BLOCK ONE**

1. Sew 2" x 6" Fabric A strips in pairs to make five 3½" x 6" strip sets. Press seams toward darker fabrics. Using rotary cutter and ruler, cut two 2" strip segments from each strip set.

2

3½

Cut 2   Make 5
strip sets

2. Sew matching segments into pairs as shown. Make five units. Press.

Make 5

3. Sew one unit from step 2 between two matching 2" x 3½" Fabric B strips. Press toward Fabric B strips. Make five.

3½
2

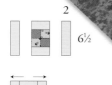

Make 5

4. Sew one unit from step 3 between two matching 2" x 6½" Fabric B strips. Press seams toward Fabric B strips. Make five. Block will measure 6½" square.

2

6½

Make 5

BLOCK TWO

1. Sew one 3½" Fabric C square between two matching 2" x 3½" Fabric D strips. Press seams toward Fabric D strips. Make eight.

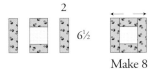

3½
2
3½

Make 8

2. Sew one unit from step 1 between two matching 2" x 6½" Fabric D strips. Press seams toward Fabric D strips. Make eight. Block will measure 6½" square.

2
6½

Make 8

3. Refer to project layout on page 84 and Embroidery Stitch Guide on page 216. Use three strands of embroidery floss and a running stitch to embroider a cross through center of each Fabric C square, creating an embroidered four-patch.

ASSEMBLY

1. Refer to diagram below. Arrange, alternating Block One and Block Two units in five rows, staggering rows as shown.

2. Sew blocks together into rows. Press seams in opposite directions from row to row.

3. Sew rows together, stopping and starting with a backstitch ¼" from raw edges. Press.

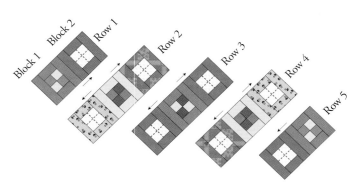

Block 1 Block 2 Row 1 Row 2 Row 3 Row 4 Row 5

LAYERING AND FINISHING

1. Position top and backing right sides together. Center both pieces on top of batting and pin all three layers together. Using ¼" seam, sew around angled edges of top, leaving an opening for turning.

2. Trim backing and batting to same size as top. Trim corners, turn right side out, hand stitch opening closed, and press.

3. Machine or hand quilt as desired.

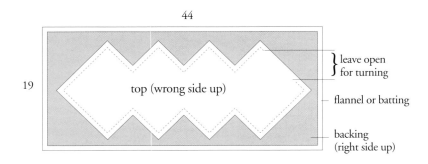

44

19

top (wrong side up)

} leave open for turning

flannel or batting

backing (right side up)

MEET OUR
KITCHEN ANGEL

*Do you ever wish you had just
a little good luck in the
kitchen when you're creating
that chocolate soufflé? Now
you have it! Our very special
Kitchen Angel is here to dust
your kitchen with a generous
sprinkling of good luck!*

*Bringing her into your cozy
kitchen setting will make
everything just a little
better … your cookies will
be done just right in the
middle, your salads crisp
and fresh, and your
pasta perfectly "al dente."
Here's a little advice:
Don't throw away your
timer … just in case!*

LITTLE WALL QUILTS

Checks and Dashes

Cutting Corners

Each Finished Quilt Size: 11" square

Photo: page 79

Nine Patch

DON'T BE FOOLED BY THEIR LITTLE

measurements! This trio of diminutive quilts delivers a large serving of decorative impact … in record time. Betcha can't make just one! Read all instructions before beginning and use ¼"-wide seams throughout.

FABRIC REQUIREMENTS

	Checks and Dashes	Nine Patch	Cutting Corners
Fabric A	⅙ yard *(center and checkerboard)*	One 4½" square *(center)*	One 6½" square *(center)*
Fabric B	⅛ yard *(checkerboard and border)*	⅛ yard *(nine-patch center and borders)*	¼ yard *(second strips and borders)*
Fabric C	⅛ yard *(background)*	⅛ yard *(nine-patch corner blocks and strip sets)*	¼ yard *(first strips and corners)*
Fabric D	⅛ yard *(inside corners)*	⅛ yard *(nine-patch corner blocks and strip sets)*	⅛ yard *(center triangles)*
For each quilt:	✳ Backing - 15" square ✳ Lightweight batting - 15" square piece ✳ Embroidery floss		

CUTTING THE STRIPS AND PIECES

	Checks and Dashes	Nine Patch	Cutting Corners
Fabric A	One 4½" square Two 1½" x16" strips		
Fabric B	Two 1½" x 16" strips Two 1" x 10½" strips Two 1" x 11½" strips	One 1½" x 8" strip Two 1" x 10½" strips Two 1" x 11½" strips	One 8½" square Two 1" x 10½" strips Two 1" x 11½" strips
Fabric C	One 3½" x 16" strip cut into • Four 3½" squares One 1½" x 20" strip cut into • Four 1½" x 4½" pieces	Two 1½" x 42" strips cut into • Two 1½" x 20" strips • One 1½" x 16" strip • Two 1½" x 8" strips	One 1½" x 42" strip cut into • Two 1½" x 8½" strips • Two 1½" x 6½" strips One 3½" x 42" strip cut into • Four 3½" squares
Fabric D	One 3½" x 42" strip cut into • Four 3½" squares	Two 1½" x 42" strips cut into • One 1½" x 20" strip • Two 1½" x 16" strips	One 3½" x 42" strip cut into • Four 3½" squares

CHECKS AND DASHES

1. Alternate fabric and sew two 1½" x 16" Fabric A and Fabric B strips together to make one 4½" x 16" strip set. Press seams toward darker fabrics. Using rotary cutter and ruler, cut eight 1½" segments from strip set.

1½

4½

Cut 8

2. Sew segments in pairs as shown to make four units. Press. Then sew one 1½" x 4½" Fabric C piece to each unit. Press.

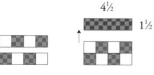

4½

1½

Make 4

3. Refer to Quick Corner Triangle directions on page 216. Using 3½" Fabric C and Fabric D squares, make four units. Press.

C = 3½ x 3½
D = 3½ x 3½
Make 4

4. Sew one unit from step 2 between two units from step 3. Press. Make two.

Make 2

5. Sew 4½" Fabric A square between remaining units from step 2. Press.

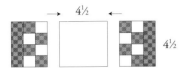

4½

4½

6. Sew unit from step 5 between units from step 4 as shown. Press. Block will measure 10½" square.

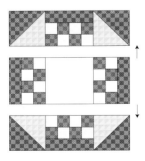

7. Sew 1" x 10½" Fabric B strips to top and bottom of block. Press seams toward border strips. Sew 1" x 11½" strips to sides. Press.

8. Trace embroidery pattern on page 93 onto Fabric A block center. Refer to Embroidery Stitch Guide on page 216. Use embroidery floss to embroider as desired.

LAYERING AND FINISHING

1. Position top and backing right sides together. Center both pieces on top of batting and pin all three layers together. Using ¼" seam, sew around edges leaving an opening for turning.

2. Trim backing and batting to same size as top. Trim corners, turn right side out, hand stitch opening closed, and press.

3. Machine or hand quilt as desired.

NINE PATCH

1. Sew 1½" x 8" Fabric B strip between two 1½" x 8" Fabric C strips to make one 3½" x 8" strip set. Press seams toward darker fabrics. Using rotary cutter and ruler, cut four 1½" segments from strip set.

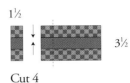

1½

3½

Cut 4

2. Sew one 1½" x 16" Fabric C strip between two 1½" x 16" Fabric D strips to make one 3½" x 16" strip set. Press seams toward darker fabrics. Using rotary cutter and ruler, cut eight 1½" segments from strip set.

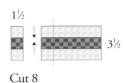

1½

3½

Cut 8

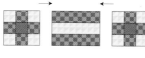

3. Sew one unit from step 1 between two units from step 2 as shown. Press. Make four.

Make 4

4. Sew one 1½" x 20" Fabric D strip between two 1½" x 20" Fabric C strips to make one 3½" x 20" strip set. Press. Using rotary cutter and ruler, cut four 4½" segments from strip set.

4½

3½

Cut 4

5. Sew one unit from step 4 between two units from step 3. Press. Make two.

Make 2

6. Sew 4½" Fabric A square between remaining units from step 4. Press.

4½

4½

7. Sew unit from step 6 between units from step 5 as shown. Press.

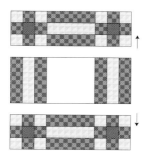

8. Sew 1" x 10½" Fabric B strips to top and bottom of block. Press seams toward border strips. Sew 1" x 11½" strips to sides. Press.

9. Trace embroidery pattern on page 93 onto Fabric A block center. Refer to Embroidery Stitch Guide on page 216. Use embroidery floss to embroider as desired.

10. Follow steps 1-3 of Layering and Finishing for the Checks and Dashes Little Wall Quilts on page 90.

MIX THE OLD WITH THE NEW

Mixing the old with the new can be a winning combination. For a delightful decorating touch, mix your lovely new dinnerware with vintage kitchen collectibles. If you're not already a seasoned collector, kitchen goodies are an ideal place to start. The choices are abundant … pottery bowls, colorful tinware, wire utensils, vintage table linens, and the possibilities go on and on. And the best part? Many are still affordable and can be found in a variety of places such as flea markets, garage sales, and antique shops just to name a few.

Go ahead … mix it up! The surprising contrast between the precious old and the shiny new will bring your own personal look to your kitchen.

CUTTING CORNERS

1. Refer to Quick Corner Triangle directions on page 216. Sew four 3½" Fabric D squares to 6½" center square. Press.

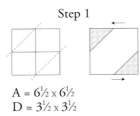

Step 1

A = 6½ x 6½
D = 3½ x 3½

Step 2

D = 3½ x 3½

2. Sew 1½" x 6½" Fabric C strips to top and bottom. Press toward strip. Then sew 1½" x 8½" Fabric C strips to sides. Press.

3. Cut 8½" Fabric B square in half twice diagonally to make four triangles.

4. Sew one triangle to each side of unit from step 2. Press. Carefully trim block to 10½" square. Be sure Fabric A square is centered in the block. (Trimming will cut off blue points.)

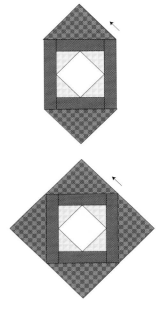

5. Refer to Quick Corner Triangle directions on page 216. Sew four 3½" Fabric C corner squares to unit from step 4. Press. Block will measure 10½" square.

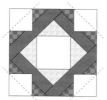

C = 3½ x 3½

6. Sew 1" x 10½" Fabric B strips to top and bottom of block. Sew 1" x 11½" strips to sides. Press seams toward border strips.

7. Trace embroidery pattern from this page onto Fabric A block center. Refer to Embroidery Stitch Guide on page 216. Use embroidery floss to embroider as desired.

8. Follow steps 1-3 of Layering and Finishing for the Checks and Dashes Little Wall Quilts on page 90.

toaster embroidery pattern for Cutting Corners

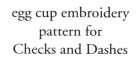

coffee pot embroidery pattern for shelf doilies

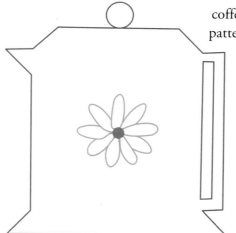

egg cup embroidery pattern for Checks and Dashes

teapot embroidery pattern for Nine Patch

BEAUTIFUL BUTTERFLIES

LOOK CLOSELY AND *you'll see them fluttering through the soft rays of summer sunshine. These beautiful butterflies invite you into a sweet-smelling garden to relax and enjoy the gorgeous blooms all around.*

What a delightful setting for a light lunch ... or just for sitting back, fluffing your pillow, and passing a lazy afternoon among fragrant flowers and delicate butterflies.

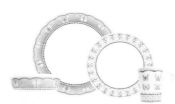

BUTTERFLY DINNERWARE

BUTTERFLY GARDEN QUILT

Finished Size: 58" x 82"

Photo: page 94

DELICATE EMBROIDERED BUTTERFLIES HOVER

over carefully-tended "flower beds" in this colorful patchwork garden. We made this project in an assortment of our pretty pastels, but it will be lovely in any color scheme. Read all instructions before beginning and use ¼"-wide seams throughout.

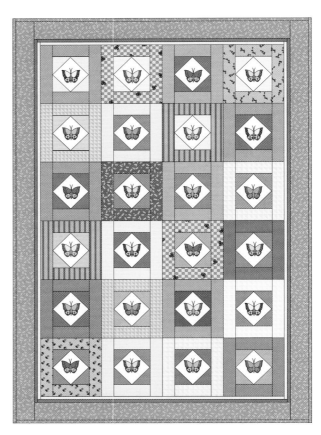

Quilt Layout

FABRIC REQUIREMENTS

Fabric A *(block centers)* - ⅞ yard light fabric

Fabric B *(corner triangles)* - Four 3½" squares each of twenty-four assorted scrappy fabrics

Fabric C *(block frames)* - One 3½" x 42" strip each of twenty-four assorted scrappy fabrics

First Accent Border - ¼ yard

Second Accent Border - ¼ yard

Border - ⅞ yard

Binding - ¾ yard

Backing - 3⅝ yards

Lightweight batting 66" x 90" piece

Embroidery floss or thread

Butterfly embroidery -

Debbie Mumm® Every Day machine embroidery card from Bernina of America, (888) BERNINA

CUTTING THE STRIPS AND PIECES

Read first paragraph of Cutting the Strips and Pieces on page 5.

Fabric A (block centers)
* Four 6½" x 42" strips, cut into
  * Twenty-four 6½" squares

Fabric C (block frames)
* Two 3½" x 12½" strips
* Two 3½" x 6½" strips

Repeat for each of twenty-four strips.

First Accent Border
* Seven 1" x 42" strips

Second Accent Border
* Seven 1" x 42" strips

Border
* Seven 4" x 42" strips

Binding
* Eight 2¾" x 42" strips

MAKING THE BLOCKS

You'll be making twenty-four framed Diamond in a Square Blocks.

Whenever possible, use the assembly line method for each step. Position pieces right sides together and line up next to your sewing machine. Stitch first unit together, then continue sewing others without breaking threads. When all units are sewn, clip threads to separate them. Press in direction of arrows in diagrams.

1. Refer to Quick Corner Triangle directions on page 216. Sew four matching 3½" Fabric B squares to each 6½" Fabric A square. Press. Make a total of twenty-four.

Step 1

A = 6½ x 6½
B = 3½ x 3½
Make 24

Step 2

Make 24

2. Sew one unit from above between two matching 3½" x 6½" Fabric C strips. Press. Make a total of twenty-four.

6½

3½

Make 24

3. Sew one unit from step 2 between two matching 3½" x 12½" Fabric C strips. Press. Make a total of twenty-four. Block will measure 12½".

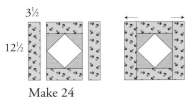

Make 24

4. Machine embroider butterfly pattern or trace embroidery pattern below onto Fabric A block center. Refer to Embroidery Stitch Guide on page 216. Use embroidery floss to embroider as desired.

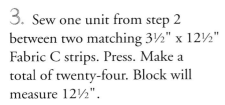

ASSEMBLY

1. Refer to project layout on page 96. Arrange blocks in pleasing arrangement of six horizontal rows with four blocks each. Sew blocks into rows. Press seams in opposite directions from row to row.

2. Sew rows together. Press.

3. Cut one 1" x 42" first accent border strip in half and sew a half strip to two first accent border strips. Measure quilt through center from side to side. Trim strips to this measurement. Sew to top and bottom. Press toward accent border.

4. Sew remaining 1" x 42" first accent border strips together in pairs. Measure quilt through center from top to bottom. Trim strips to this measurement. Sew to sides. Press.

5. Repeat steps 3 and 4 for second accent border.

6. Measure, trim, and add 4" borders to quilt in same manner.

LAYERING AND FINISHING

1. Cut backing fabric crosswise into two equal pieces. Sew pieces together on long edges to make one 65" x 90" (approximate) backing piece. Arrange and baste backing, batting, and top together, referring to Layering the Quilt directions on page 217.

2. Hand or machine quilt as desired.

3. Cut two 2¾" x 42" binding strips in half. Sew one half to each of two 2¾" x 42" strips. Sew remaining 2¾" x 42" binding strips together in pairs and sew one remaining half to each strip. Using shorter strips for top and bottom and longer strips for sides, refer to Binding the Quilt directions on page 217 to finish.

butterfly embroidery patterns for Butterfly Garden Quilt and Flutter By Pillow

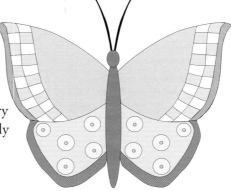

BUTTERFLY DINNERWARE

Create a perfect setting for warm sunny days with this charming melamine dinnerware adorned with delicate butterflies in shades of soft blues and yellows. For information on where to buy Debbie Mumm® dinnerware, visit www.debbiemumm.com or call (888) 819-2923.

FLUTTER BY

PILLOW

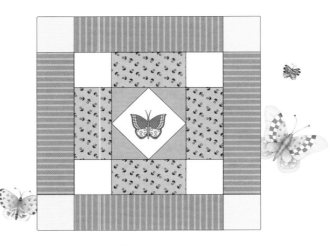

Pillow Layout

Finished Size: 16" square

Photo: page 99

PAIR THIS PASTEL PRETTY WITH

the matching Butterfly Garden Quilt, or place it center stage on a sofa, rocker, or easy chair. Read all instructions before beginning and use ¼"-wide seams throughout.

FABRIC REQUIREMENTS

Fabric A *(block center)* - One 6½" square of light fabric

Fabric B *(corner triangles)* - Four 3½" squares

Inside Border - ⅛ yard

Inside Corner Squares - Four 3" squares

Outside Border - ⅙ yard

Outside Corner Squares - Four 3" squares

Lining - 20" square

Batting - 20" square

Backing - ⅓ yard

Pillow form - 16" square

Embroidery floss

CUTTING THE STRIPS AND PIECES

Read first paragraph of Cutting the Strips and Pieces on page 5.

Inside Border

* One 3" x 42" strip, cut into
  • Four 3" x 6½" pieces

Outside Border

* Two 3" x 42" strips, cut into
  • Four 3" x 11½" pieces

Backing

* One 11" x 42" strip, cut into
  • Two 11" x 16½" pieces

MAKING THE BLOCK

1. Refer to Quick Corner Triangle directions on page 216. Sew four 3½" Fabric B squares to opposite sides of 6½" Fabric A square. Press.

Step 1 Step 2

A = 6½ x 6½
B = 3½ x 3½
B = 3½ x 3½

2. Sew unit from above between two 3" x 6½" inside border strips. Press seams toward border strips.

6½
3

3. Sew each remaining 3" x 6½" inside border strip between two 3" inside corner squares. Press.

6½
3

Make 2

4. Sew unit from step 2 between units from step 3. Press.

5. Sew unit from step 4 between two 3" x 11½" outside border strips. Press.

3

11½

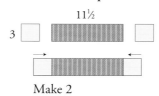

6. Sew each remaining 3" x 11½" outside border strip between two 3" outside corner squares. Press.

11½
3

Make 2

7. Sew unit from step 5 between units from step 6. Press.

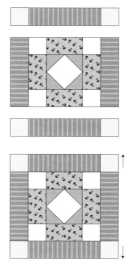

8. Machine embroider or trace embroidery pattern from page 98 onto Fabric A block center. Refer to Embroidery Stitch Guide on page 216. Use embroidery floss to embroider as desired.

9. Layer batting between top and lining. Baste. Hand or machine quilt as desired.

LAYERING AND FINISHING

1. Narrow hem one long edge of each 11" x 16½" backing piece by folding under ¼" to wrong side. Press. Fold again ¼" to wrong side. Topstitch along folded edge.

2. With right sides up, lay one backing piece over second piece so hemmed edges overlap, making single 16½" backing panel. Baste pieces together at top and bottom where they overlap. Refer to diagrams on page 36.

3. With right sides together, position and pin pillow top to backing. Using ¼" seam, sew around edges. Trim corners, turn right side out, and press.

4. Insert pillow form into pillow cover.

Finished Size: 18" x 19½"

Photo: page 104

FAMILY AND FRIENDS WILL FEEL MORE THAN

welcome when greeted by this colorful banner in your kitchen, entry, or hall. We used nine different colors of felted wool and three different colors of embroidery floss to create the quick-fuse appliqués, but you may use as few or as many as you'd like.

Banner Layout

FABRIC REQUIREMENTS

Background - 16" x 18" piece of felted wool

Backing - Two 18½" x 22½" panels of coordinating cotton fabric (⅔ yard)

Assorted felted wool scraps for appliqués and tabs

Notions:

- 1 yard of sewable fusible web
- Embroidery floss in assorted colors

- Dowel - ⅜" - diameter, 15" length
- Two end caps for dowel
- Acrylic paint
- Buttons - fourteen ⅜"- diameter in coordinating colors, two ¾"- diameter porcelain

[Porcelain buttons by Porcelain Rose, (562) 424-9728]

ASSEMBLING THE BACKGROUND PANEL

1. Measure down 6" from the top along the left and right sides of one 18½" x 22½" cotton panel. Mark these measurements.

2. Measure 6" across top from both left and right upper corners on same cotton panel. Mark these measurements.

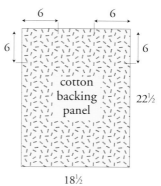

cotton backing panel

18½

3. Angle a ruler across one corner, using marked measurements as a guide. Use your rotary cutter to trim corner. Repeat for other corner.

cotton backing panel

18½

4. Repeat steps 1-3 to measure, mark, and trim second 18½" x 22½" cotton backing panel.

5. Position trimmed cotton backing panels right sides together. Using ¼" seam, sew around edges, leaving a 3" opening for turning. Trim corners, turn right side out, hand stitch opening closed, and press.

6. Repeat steps 1-3 to measure, mark, and trim a 3" triangle from top corners of 16" x 18" felted wool panel as shown.

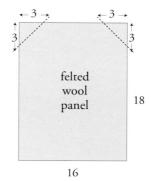

felted wool panel

16

QUICK-FUSE APPLIQUÉ

1. Refer to Quick-Fuse Appliqué directions on page 217. Use patterns on pages 105-106. Reverse those that are marked on pattern pieces and trace one each of pattern piece 9 and letters W, L, C, O, and M; two of letter E; and six each of pattern pieces 10 and 11 onto paper side of fusible web.

In addition, trace one regular and one reverse each of pattern pieces 1-6, 7a-h, and 8. Note: Piece 6 is the large background piece for checkerboard.

FELTED WOOL

*It's simple to give
your wool an
added richness and
fullness … felt it!*

*The easiest way to do
this is to put it through
the wash cycle on your
washing machine
using hot water.*

*After washing, put it
into the dryer until
it is thoroughly dry.
The result will be
a thicker, fuller fabric
that will give
added texture to
your Welcome Banner.*

2. Quick-fuse butterfly layers, referring to layout on page 102 for guidance. In similar fashion, quick-fuse one small background circle to each large background circle.

3. Quick-fuse layered butterfly, layered circles, and WELCOME letters to wool panel, referring to layout on page 102 for placement.

4. Refer to Embroidery Stitch Guide on page 216. Use six strands of embroidery floss to blanket stitch around butterfly, wing checkerboard, and other appliqués as desired. Use three strands of floss to stem stitch antennae.

5. Position appliquéd wool panel face up on backing panel. Backing should extend ½" beyond bottom edge, 1" beyond side edges, and 2" beyond top edge of wool panel as shown. Refer to Embroidery Stitch Guide on page 216 . Use six strands of embroidery floss to blanket stitch wool panel to backing panel.

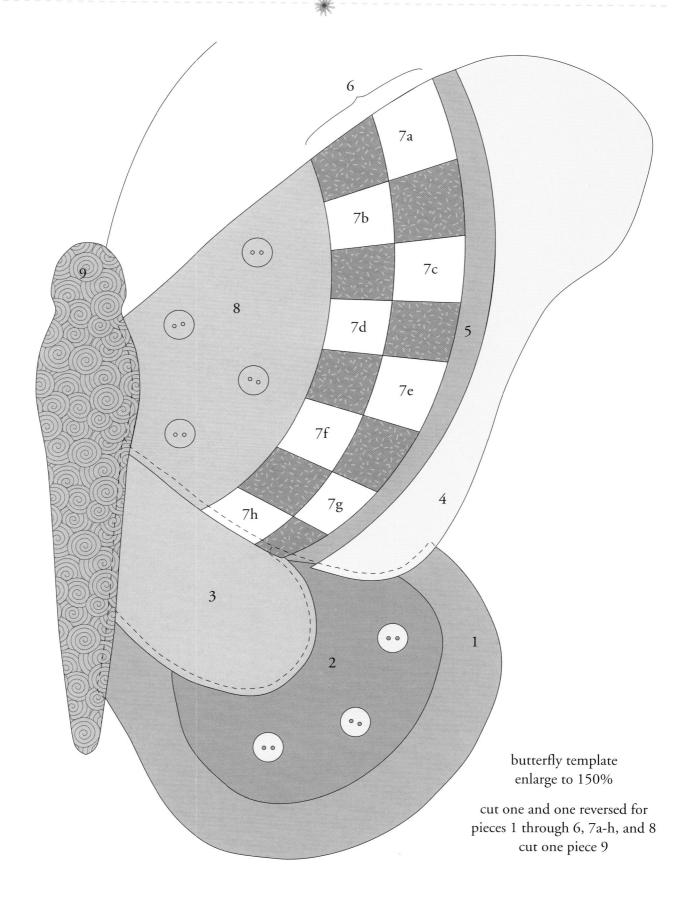

6

7a

7b

7c

7d

7e

7f

7g

7h

9

8

5

4

3

2

1

butterfly template
enlarge to 150%

cut one and one reversed for
pieces 1 through 6, 7a-h, and 8
cut one piece 9

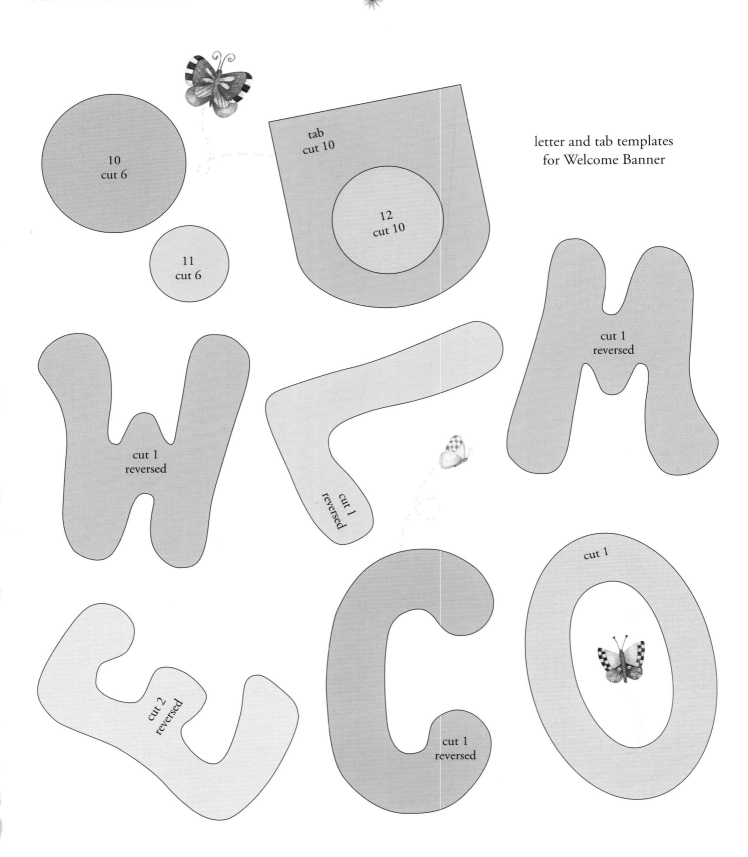

10
cut 6

11
cut 6

tab
cut 10

12
cut 10

letter and tab templates
for Welcome Banner

cut 1
reversed

cut 1
reversed

cut 1
reversed

cut 1
reversed

cut 2
reversed

cut 1
reversed

cut 1

FINISHING THE BANNER

1. Use tab pattern on page 106 to make template and trace ten tabs from remaining wool scraps.

2. Turn top edge of backing to front side of wool panel.

3. Appliqué bottom edge of turned backing panel to banner front.

4. With right sides together, sew two wool tabs to top edge of backed panel as shown. Flip tabs, add two pattern piece 12 felt circles with blanket stitch, and secure with ¾"-diameter porcelain buttons, stitching through all layers of banner "sandwich."

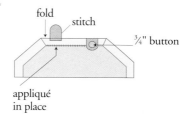

fold
stitch
¾" button
appliqué in place

5. Refer to Quick-Fuse Appliqué directions on page 217. Trace and cut eight of pattern piece 12 onto paper side of fusible web. Quick-fuse to remaining wool tabs.

6. Whip stitch fused tabs to bottom edge of banner backing. Refer to layout on page 102 for guidance. Blanket stitch around tabs and circles.

7. Sew through all layers to attach ⅜"-diameter buttons to butterfly wings. Refer to layout on page 102 for guidance.

8. Paint dowel and dowel end caps with acrylic paint in coordinating color. Allow to dry and slip through top flap.

Debbie Mumm's®
BIRDHOUSES FOR EVERY SEASON

Our favorite feathered friends settle into their backyard birdhouse homes during every season of the year in this collection of more than twenty charming quilts and decorating projects. Cheerful birds, friendly ladybugs, and graceful butterflies join in flights of fancy on these easy projects, perfect for every room of your home.

Spring

Beautiful birds and butterflies ... every year they announce that wonderfully welcome spring has finally arrived!

Soon our favorite feathered friends will settle into their backyard birdhouse homes and fluttering butterflies will join in the springtime welcome with their flights of fancy in and out of the fragrant blossoms.

This delightful vision of spring doesn't have to stay just in the garden. Bring the birdhouse whimsy indoors, too, with blooming-fresh projects created in the soft-as-a-breeze shades of spring.

Trellis in Bloom Bed Quilt

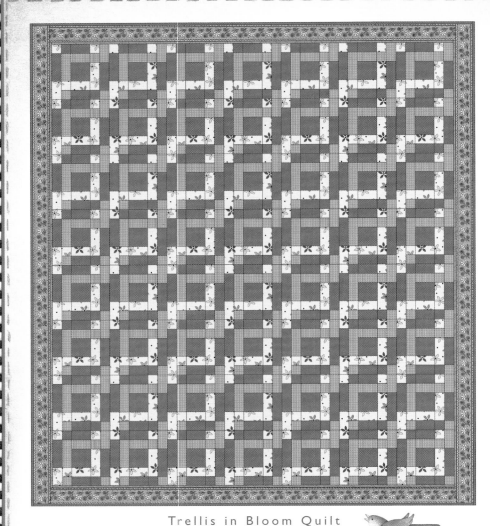

Bring the fresh
colors and ordered elegance of a
traditional English garden indoors
as you spread this blooming creation
atop a waiting bed.

Simple to piece,
this generously-sized quilt is
created with a single repeating block!
Read all instructions before beginning and
use ¼"-wide seam allowances
throughout.

Trellis in Bloom Quilt
Finished Size: 93" x 105"
Photo: page 110

FABRIC REQUIREMENTS

Fabric A - 2¾ yards
Fabric B - 4¼ yards
Fabric C - 2¾ yards
Accent Border - ⅓ yard
Border - 1¼ yards*
Binding - ⅞ yard
Backing - 8⅛ yards
Lightweight Batting - 101" x 113"

*If you select a border print as we
   did, you will need to increase the
   yardage, depending on the number
      of design repeats in the fabric.

CUTTING THE STRIPS AND PIECES

Pre-wash and press fabrics. Using rotary cutter, see-through ruler, and cutting mat, cut the following strips and pieces. If indicated, some will need to be cut again into smaller strips and pieces. The approximate width of the fabric is 42". Measurements for all pieces include ¼"-wide seam allowance. Press in the direction of arrows.

		Number of Strips	Dimensions
	FABRIC A	4	4½" x 42"
		19	2½" x 42"
		4	6½" x 42"
	FABRIC B	22	2½" x 42"
		8	6½" x 42"
		7	4½" x 42"
	FABRIC C	4	4½" x 42"
		19	2½" x 42"
		4	6½" x 42"
	ACCENT BORDER	10	1" x 42"
	BORDER	10	4" x 42"
	BINDING	10	2¾" x 42"

MAKING THE BLOCKS

You will be making 56 lattice blocks. See Assembly Line Method on page 5, and use whenever possible.

1. Sew one 6½" x 42" Fabric B strip between one 2½" x 42" Fabric A strip and one 4½" x 42" Fabric A strip to make four 12½" x 42" strip sets as shown. Press. Using rotary cutter and ruler, cut fifty-six 2½" segments from strip sets. Label them unit 1.

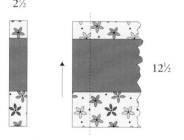

2½

12½

unit 1
Make 4 strip sets
Cut 56

2. Sew one 2½" x 42" Fabric B strip, one 6½" x 42" Fabric C strip, one 2½" x 42" Fabric A strip, and one 2½" x 42" Fabric C strip in order shown to make four 12½" x 42" strip sets. Press. Using rotary cutter and ruler, cut fifty-six 2½" segments from strip sets. Label them unit 2.

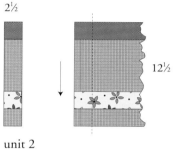

2½

12½

unit 2
Make 4 strip sets
Cut 56

3. Sew one 2½" x 42" Fabric B strip, one 2½" x 42" Fabric C strip, one 4½" x 42" Fabric B strip, one 2½" x 42" Fabric A strip, and one 2½" x 42" Fabric B strip in order shown to make seven 12½" x 42" strip sets. Press. Using rotary cutter and ruler, cut fifty-six 4½" segments from strip sets. Label them unit 3.

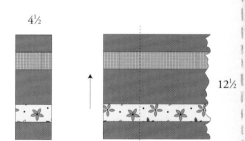

4½

12½

unit 3
Make 7 strip sets
Cut 56

4. Sew one 2½" x 42" Fabric A strip, one 2½" x 42" Fabric C strip, one 6½" x 42" Fabric A strip, and one 2½" x 42" Fabric B strip in order shown to make four 12½" x 42" strip sets. Press. Using rotary cutter and ruler, cut fifty-six 2½" segments from strip sets. Label them unit 4.

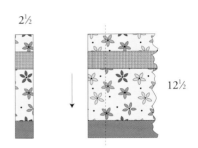

2½

12½

unit 4
Make 4 strip sets
Cut 56

5. Sew one 4½" x 42" Fabric C strip, one 6½" x 42" Fabric B strip, and one 2½" x 42" Fabric C strip in order shown to make four 12½" x 42" strip sets. Press. Using rotary cutter and ruler, cut fifty-six 2½" segments from strip sets. Label them unit 5.

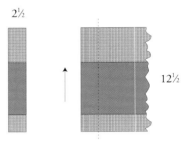

2½

12½

unit 5
Make 4 strip sets
Cut 56

6. Arrange and sew units 1 through 5 as shown. Make 56 blocks. Press 28 blocks toward unit 5 and 28 blocks toward unit 1. Block will measure 12½" square.

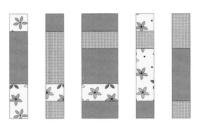

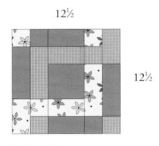

12½

12½

Make 56

ASSEMBLY

1. Refer to layout on page 112 and color photo. Arrange blocks in eight horizontal rows of seven blocks each. Sew blocks into rows. Press seams in opposite directions from row to row.

2. Sew rows together. Press.

3. Sew 1" x 42" accent border strips end to end to make one continuous 1" strip. Measure quilt from side to side through center. Cut two 1"-wide accent border strips to that measurement. Sew to top and bottom. Press seams toward border strips.

4. Measure quilt through center from top to bottom, including borders just added. Cut two 1"-wide border strips to that measurement. Sew to sides. Press.

5. Sew 4" x 42" border strips end to end to make one continuous 4"-wide strip. Measure quilt through center from side to side. Cut two 4"-wide border strips to that measurement. Sew to top and bottom. Press seams toward border strips.

6. Measure quilt through center from top to bottom, including borders just added. Cut two 4"-wide border strips to that measurement. Sew to sides. Press.

LAYERING AND FINISHING

1. Cut backing fabric crosswise into three equal pieces. Sew pieces together to make one 98" x 120" (approximate) backing piece. Arrange and baste backing, batting, and top together, referring to Layering the Quilt directions on page 217.

2. Machine or hand quilt as desired.

3. Sew eight 2¾" x 42" binding strips together in pairs. Cut two remaining strips in half and sew halves to each pieced strip. Refer to Binding the Quilt directions on page 217 to finish.

Birdhouse Pillow Covers

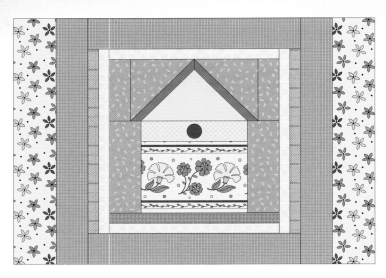

Birdhouse Pillow Covers
Finished Size: 34" x 24"
Photo: page 110

You'll love this *perky pillow cover with its morning-fresh colors and crisp flanged edges. It pairs up perfectly with our lovely Trellis in Bloom Bed Quilt, but you can display it anyplace you want to spread a touch of spring.*

Instructions here are *for a single sham, but they're so quick and easy you'll want to make more than one! Read all instructions before beginning, and use ¼"-wide seams throughout.*

FABRIC REQUIREMENTS

Fabric A (Background) - ¼ yard
Fabric B (Upper House) - ¼ yard
Fabric C (Middle House) - ⅛ yard
Fabric D (Lower House) - ¼ yard
Fabric E (Grass) - ⅛ yard
Roof Appliqués - ⅛ yard
Birdhouse Hole Appliqué - Scrap

Accent Border - ⅛ yard
Second Border - ⅛ yard
Third Border - ⅓ yard
Outside Border - ⅜ yard
Back Panels - 1⅜ yards
Lining - ⅞ yard
Lightweight Batting - 38" x 28" piece

CUTTING THE STRIPS AND PIECES

Read first paragraph of Cutting the Strips and Pieces on page 5.

	FIRST CUT		SECOND CUT	
	Number of Strips or Pieces	Dimensions	Number of Pieces	Dimensions
FABRIC A	2 2 2	6½" squares 2½" x 6½" 3½" x 9½"		
FABRIC B	1	12½" x 6½"		
FABRIC C	1	10½" x 2½"		
FABRIC D	1	10½" x 7½"		
FABRIC E	1	1½" x 16½"		
ROOF APPLIQUÉ	2	1¼" x 9½"		
ACCENT BORDER	2	1½" x 42"	2 2	1½" x 16½" 1½" x 18½"
SECOND BORDER	1	1½" x 42"	2	1½" x 18½"
THIRD BORDER	3	3½" x 42"	2 2	3½" x 20½" 3½" x 24½"
OUTSIDE BORDER	2	4½" x 42"	2	4½" x 24½"
BACK PANELS	2	24½" x 22½"		
LINING	1	38" x 28" piece		

BLOCK ASSEMBLY

You'll be making one birdhouse block. Whenever possible, use the Assembly Line Method on page 5.

1. Refer to Quick Corner Triangle directions on page 216. Sew two 6½" Fabric A squares to 12½" x 6½" Fabric B piece as shown. Press.

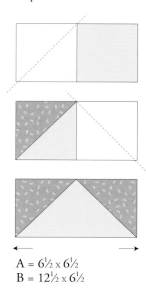

A = 6½ x 6½
B = 12½ x 6½

2. Sew unit from step 1 between two 2½" x 6½" Fabric A pieces. Press.

2½   2½   6½

3. Sew 10½" x 2½" Fabric C piece to 10½" x 7½" Fabric D piece as shown. Press.

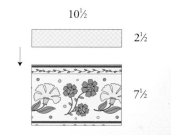

10½

2½

7½

APPLIQUÉ

1. Trace appliqué design from page 143. Make template and use scrap to cut one of birdhouse hole #2. Cut out appliqué, adding ¼" seam allowance.

2. Machine stitch or refer to Hand Appliqué directions on page 216. Appliqué two 1¼" x 9½" roof strips over roof. Follow seam lines, and square ends as shown. Refer to layout on page 116 and appliqué birdhouse hole to middle house strip.

PILLOW COVER ASSEMBLY

1. Layer batting between top and lining. Baste. Hand or machine quilt as desired. Trim batting and lining even with raw edge of sham top.

2. Machine stitch ¼"-wide hem along one 24½" edge of each 24½" x 22½" back panel. Fold hemmed edges 3" to wrong side and pin.

4. Sew unit from step 3 between two 3½" x 9½" Fabric A pieces. Press.

3½   3½

9½

5. Refer to layout on page 116. Arrange and sew unit from step 2, unit from step 4, and 1½" x 16½" Fabric E strip in order shown to make a vertical row.

BORDERS

1. Sew 1½" x 16½" accent border strips to top and bottom of block. Press seams toward borders. Sew 1½" x 18½" accent border strips to sides. Press.

2. Sew 1½" x 18½" second border strips to sides. Press seams away from center block.

3. Sew 3½" x 20½" third border strips to top and bottom. Press away from center block. Sew 3½" x 24½" third border strips to sides. Press.

4. Sew 4½" x 24½" outside border strips to sides. Press away from center block.

3. With right sides facing up, layer hemmed edges of backing pieces and overlap so that back measures 34½" x 24½" as shown. Baste pieces together along top and bottom edges where they overlap.

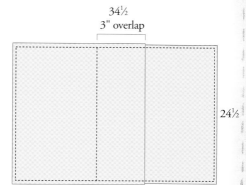

4. With right sides together, pin quilted sham top to backing. Sew all around outside edges with ¼"-wide seam. Trim corners, turn right side out, and press.

5. Refer to layout on page 116. Topstitch 3" from finished edge all around perimeter of sham as shown.

6. Insert pillow through opening in sham backing.

Small Pillow Covers

Use this smaller version of our Birdhouse Pillow Covers to create delightful decorative pillows for your bed. Finished size will be 20" x 18". Photo on cover.

FABRIC REQUIREMENTS

Follow fabric requirements for Birdhouse Pillow Covers Fabric A through Second Border.
Lining - ⅔ yard
Backing Panels - ⅜ yard
Pillow Form - 18"
Batting - 24" x 22"

CUTTING THE STRIPS AND PIECES

Follow cutting chart for Birdhouse Pillow Covers Fabric A through Second Border.
Lining
  One 24" x 22" piece
Back Panels
  Two 12½" x 18½"

BLOCK ASSEMBLY

1. You'll be making one birdhouse block following instructions beginning on page 117, steps one through five.

2. Sew 1½" x 16½" accent border strips to top and bottom of block. Press seams toward borders. Sew 1½" x 18½" accent border strips to sides. Press.

3. Sew 1½" x 18½" second border strips to sides. Press seams away from center block.

APPLIQUÉ

1. Trace appliqué design from page 143. Make template and use scrap to cut one of birdhouse hole #2. Cut out appliqué, adding ¼" seam allowance.

2. Machine stitch or refer to Hand Appliqué directions on page 216. Appliqué two 1¼" x 9½" roof pieces. Follow seam lines, and square ends as shown.

PILLOW ASSEMBLY

1. Layer batting between top and lining. Baste. Hand or machine quilt as desired. Trim batting and lining even with raw edge of pillow top.

2. Machine stitch ¼"-wide hem along one 18½" edge of each 12½" x 18½" back panel.

3. With right sides up, lay one backing piece over second piece so hemmed edges overlap, measuring 20½" x 18½". Adjust overlap to fit pillow top. Baste pieces together where they overlap.

4. With right sides together, position and pin pillow top to backing. Using ¼" seam, sew around edges. Trim corner, turn right side out, and press.

5. Top stitch between accent border and second border.

Beautiful Butterflies Wall Quilt

As softly colored *as the blossoms of spring, these delicate butterflies create a charming scene as they hover near their garden home.*

Constructed with a *variety of quick piecing techniques and completed with the simplest of appliqué and embroidery, they'll alight on your wall before you know it! Read all instructions before beginning and use ¼"-wide seams throughout.*

Beautiful Butterflies Wall Quilt
Finished Size: 40" x 41"
Photo: page 125

FABRIC REQUIREMENTS

Fabric A (Upper Wings) - eight scraps
 in a variety of colors
Fabric B (Background) - 1 yard
Fabric C (Lower Wings) - eight scraps
 in a variety of colors
Fabric D (Gable) - scrap
Fabrics E and F (Checkerboard)
 ⅛ yd of 2 contrasting fabrics
Fabric G (Gable Accent) - scrap
Fabric H (House Front) - scrap
Fabric I (Roof and Floor) - scraps
Appliqués - Assorted scraps for
 butterfly bodies and house
 openings

Inside Accent Border - ⅙ yard
Second Accent Border - ⅙ yard
Outside Border - ½ yard
Binding - ½ yard
Backing - 1¼ yards *
Lightweight Batting - 44" x 45" piece
Black Embroidery Floss or
 Perle Cotton

* Fabric must measure 45" wide.

CUTTING THE STRIPS AND PIECES

Read first paragraph of Cutting the Strips and Pieces on page 5.

	FIRST CUT		SECOND CUT	
	Number of Strips or Pieces	Dimensions	Number of Pieces	Dimensions
FABRIC A eight fabrics	12	5½" squares *		
FABRIC B	5	1½" x 42"	50 12 1 1 5	1½" squares 1½" x 5½" 1½" x 11½" 1½" x 10½" 1½" x 6½"
	1	5½" x 42"	4	5½" squares
	2	3½" x 42"	8 2 2	3½" squares 3½" x 10½" 3" squares
	3	2½" x 42"	12 5 1 2	2½" squares 2½" x 10½" 2½" x 11½" 2½" x 6½"
FABRIC C eight fabrics	4 8	3½" squares 3½" x 6½" **		
FABRIC D	1	3" x 5½"		
FABRICS E and F	1	1½" x 9" ea. (2 contrasting fabrics)		
FABRIC G	1	1" x 5½"		
FABRIC H	1	5½" square		
FABRIC I	1	1½" x 42"	1 2	1½" x 7½" 1¼" x 6"
INSIDE ACCENT BORDER	4	1" x 42"		
SECOND ACCENT BORDER	4	1" x 42"		
OUTSIDE BORDER	4	3½" x 42"		
BINDING	5	2¾" x 42"		

* Cut two each from four fabrics, one each from four other fabrics.
** Cut four to match 3½" squares.

MAKING THE BLOCKS

In addition to the butterfly house, you will be making four full butterfly blocks and four butterfly profile blocks. Butterflies (bodies and wings) are made from a variety of scrap fabrics.

Whenever possible, use the Assembly Line Method on page 5.

Full Butterfly Blocks

1. Refer to Quick Corner Triangle directions on page 216. Sew 1½" Fabric B squares to two adjacent corners of one 5½" Fabric A square. Press. Make 4 matching pairs (a total of eight units).

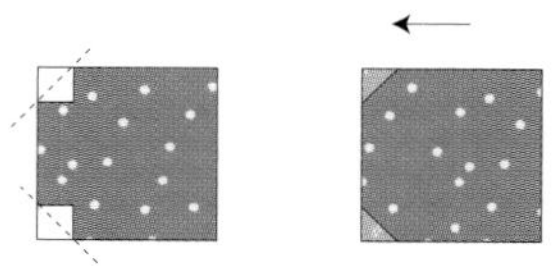

A = 5½ x 5½
B = 1½ x 1½
Make 4 matching pairs
(8 total units)

2. Sew one 2½" Fabric B square to each unit from step 1. Press. Make four of each variation shown, in matching fabric pairs.

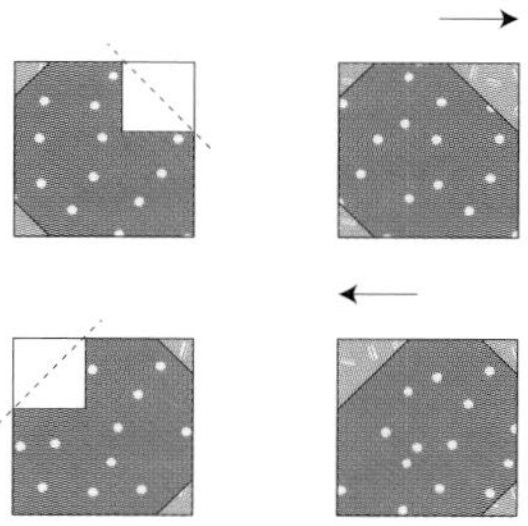

B = 2½ x 2½
Make 4 of each

3. Sew one 1½" x 5½" Fabric B piece to each unit from step 2. Press. Make four of each variation.

Make 4 of each

4. Sew 1½" Fabric B squares to two adjacent corners of each 3½" Fabric C square. Press. Make four.

B = 1½ x 1½
C = 3½ x 3½
Make 4

5. Sew one 3½" Fabric B square to each unit from step 4. Press. Make four.

3½

3½

Make 4

6. Sew 1½" Fabric B squares to two adjacent corners on the short side of each of four 3½" x 6½" Fabric C strips. Match Fabric C pieces to Fabric C squares from step 4. Press. Make four.

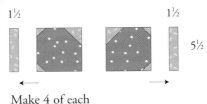

B = 1½ x 1½
C = 3½ x 6½
Make 4

7. Sew matching colored units from step 5 and step 6 in pairs as shown. Press. Make four.

Make 4

8. Arrange one of each matching colored variation from step 3, one unit from step 7, and one 5½" Fabric B square as shown. Sew the units and squares into rows. Press. Sew the rows into blocks. Press. Make four blocks.

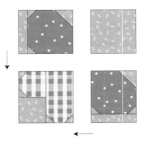

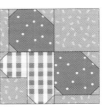

Block will measure 11½" square
Make 4

Butterfly Profile Blocks

1. Refer to Quick Corner Triangle directions on page 216. Sew 1½" Fabric B squares to two adjacent corners of remaining 5½" Fabric A squares. Press. Make two of each two variations labeling them Butterfly I and Butterfly II.

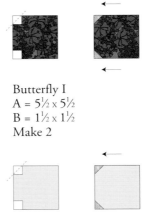

Butterfly I
A = 5½ x 5½
B = 1½ x 1½
Make 2

Butterfly II
A = 5½ x 5½
B = 1½ x 1½
Make 2

2. Sew one 2½" Fabric B square to each unit from step 1. Press. Make two of each variation.

Butterfly I
B = 2½ x 2½
Make 2

Butterfly II
B = 2½ x 2½
Make 2

3. Sew one 1½" x 5½" Fabric B piece to each unit from step 2. Press. Make two of each variation.

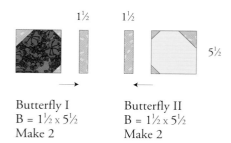

Butterfly I
B = 1½ x 5½
Make 2

Butterfly II
B = 1½ x 5½
Make 2

4. Sew 1½" Fabric B squares to two adjacent corners on one short side of remaining 3½" x 6½" Fabric C pieces. Press. Make two of each Fabric C color variation.

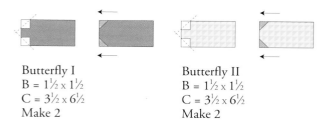

Butterfly I
B = 1½ x 1½
C = 3½ x 6½
Make 2

Butterfly II
B = 1½ x 1½
C = 3½ x 6½
Make 2

5. Sew one 3½" Fabric B square to each unit from step four. Press. Make two of each variation, labeling them Butterfly I and Butterfly II as shown.

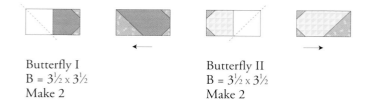

Butterfly I
B = 3½ x 3½
Make 2

Butterfly II
B = 3½ x 3½
Make 2

6. Sew units from step 3 and step 5 together, matching I and II variations as shown. Press. Make two of each block.

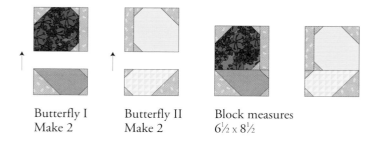

Butterfly I
Make 2

Butterfly II
Make 2

Block measures
6½ x 8½

Butterfly House Block

1. Refer to Quick Corner Triangle directions on page 216. Sew 3" Fabric B squares to 3" x 5½" Fabric D piece as shown. Press.

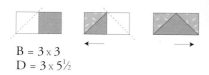

B = 3 x 3
D = 3 x 5½

2. Sew 1½" x 9" Fabric E and F strips together lengthwise. Press. Using rotary cutter and ruler, cut five 1½" segments from strip set. Arrange and sew segments to make checkerboard unit as shown. Press.

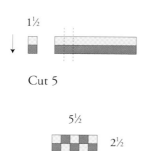

Cut 5

3. Refer to layout on page 120. Arrange and sew unit from step 1, 1" x 5½" Fabric G piece, 5½" Fabric H square, and checkerboard unit from step 3 in vertical row as shown. Press.

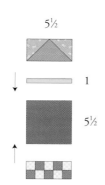

4. Sew unit from step 3 between two 2½" x 10½" Fabric B pieces. Press.

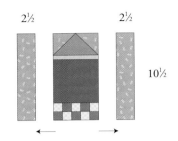

5. Sew 1½" x 7½" Fabric I piece between two 1½" Fabric B squares. Press.

6. Sew unit from step 4 to unit from step 5 as shown. Press.

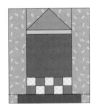

Block measures
9½ x 11½

ASSEMBLY

1. Sew two Butterfly Profile Blocks between 1½" x 6½" Fabric B pieces as shown. Press.

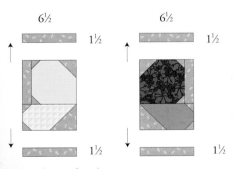

Make 1 of each

2. Sew Butterfly Profile Blocks from step 1 between one 2½" x 10½" Fabric B piece and one 3½" x 10½" Fabric B piece as shown. Press. Make one each.

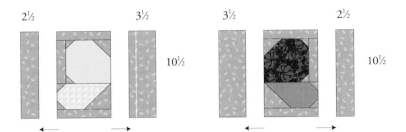

3. Refer to layout on page 120. Arrange each Butterfly Profile Block from step 2 between two full butterfly blocks in two vertical rows as shown. Sew the blocks together. Press.

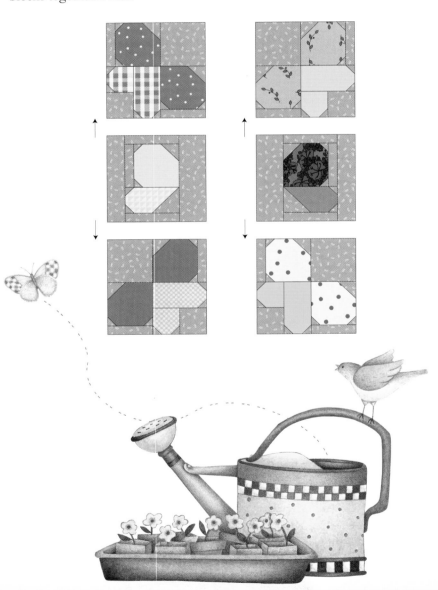

6. Sew remaining Butterfly II Profile Block between one 2½" x 6½" Fabric B piece and one 1½" x 6½" Fabric B piece as shown. Press.

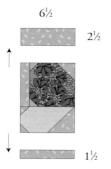

6½

2½

1½

7. Sew Butterfly II Profile Block from step 6 between one 1½" x 11½" Fabric B piece and one 2½" x 11½" Fabric B piece as shown. Press.

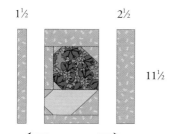

1½   2½

11½

4. Sew remaining Butterfly I Profile Block to one 2½" x 6½" Fabric B piece as shown. Press.

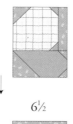

6½

2½

5. Sew Butterfly I Profile Block from step 4 between one 2½" x 10½" Fabric B piece and one 1½" x 10½" Fabric B piece as shown. Press.

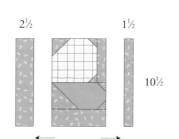

2½   1½

10½

8. Refer to layout on page 120. Arrange Butterfly House Block between Butterfly I Profile Block from step 5 and Butterfly II Profile Block from step 7 in a vertical row as shown. Sew the blocks together. Press.

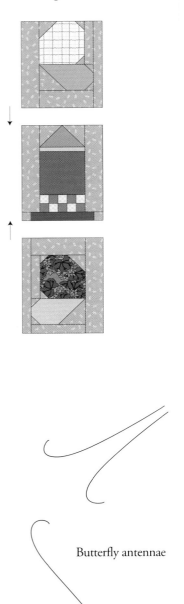

APPLIQUÉ AND EMBROIDERY

1. Refer to Quick-Fuse Applique directions on page 216. Trace appliqué designs below. Use scraps to make eight of piece 1 (butterfly body) and three of piece 2 (house opening).

Head

Piece 1

Butterfly body (Cut 8)

House opening (Cut 3)   Piece 2

Butterfly antennae

2. Refer to layout on page 120. Position one butterfly body on each full and profile butterfly block as shown. Attach bodies to wings by fusing. Satin or blanket stitch appliqués by machine or hand to secure.

3. Referring to layout and color photo, appliqué three house openings on butterfly house as shown.

4. Referring to layout and color photo, appliqué two 1¼" x 6" Fabric I roof pieces on butterfly house. Follow the seam lines and square ends as shown.

5. Refer to Embroidery Stitch Guide on page 216. Use two strands of embroidery floss to stitch antennae with a running or stem stitch to each butterfly body.

BORDERS

1. Measure quilt through center from side to side. Trim two 1" x 42" inside accent border strips to this measurement. Sew to top and bottom. Press toward accent border.

2. Measure quilt through center from top to bottom, including border. Trim remaining 1" x 42" inside accent border strips to this measurement. Sew to sides. Press.

3. Repeat steps 1 and 2 to add 1" x 42" second accent border strips to top, bottom, and sides of quilt. Press.

4. Repeat steps 1 and 2 to add 3½" x 42" outside border strips to top, bottom, and sides of quilt. Press.

LAYERING AND FINISHING

1. Arrange and baste backing, batting, and top together referring to Layering the Quilt directions on page 217.

2. Hand or machine quilt as desired.

3. Refer to Binding the Quilt directions on page 217 and use the 2¾" x 42" binding strips to finish.

Beautiful Butterflies Twin-Size Quilt

For this quilt we suggest making twenty-four full butterfly blocks using six variations in color, and adding sashing between the blocks. Below are the fabric requirements. Finished size will be 59" x 85".

FABRIC REQUIREMENTS

Fabric A (Upper Wings) - ⅓ yard
of six different fabrics
Two 5½" x 42" strips
Eight 5½" squares
Repeat for *each* color

Fabric B (Background) - 2 yards
Four 5½" x 42" strips
Twenty-four 5½" squares
Three 3½" x 42" strips
Twenty-four 3½" squares
Three 2½" x 42" strips
Forty-eight 2½" squares
Fifteen 1½" x 42" strips
One hundred ninety-two
1½" squares
Forty-eight 1½" x 5½" pieces

Fabric C (Lower Wings) - ⅛ yard
of six different fabrics
One 3½" x 42" strip
Four 3½" x 6½" pieces
Four 3½" squares

Appliqués (Body) - ⅓ yard
Cut twenty-four
Sashing - 1⅛ yards
Thirteen 2½" x 42" strips
Eighteen 2½" x 11½" pieces

Inside Accent Border - ⅓ yard
Seven 1" x 42" strips

Second Accent Border - ⅓ yard
Seven 1" x 42" strips

Outside Border - ⅞ yard
Seven 3½" x 42" strips

Binding - ⅝ yard
Seven 2¾" x 42" strips

Backing - 5⅛ yards

Lightweight Batting
67" x 93" piece

Black Embroidery Floss or
Perle Cotton

1. Refer to instructions for Full Butterfly Blocks in Beautiful Butterflies Wall Quilt on pages 121 and 122 to make four blocks of each color. Follow steps 1 through 8.

2. Arrange six horizontal rows of four blocks each. Place the 2½" x 11½" sashing pieces between the blocks in each horizontal row. Stitch together and press seams toward the sashing.

3. Cut five 12" strips from two 2½" x 42" strips and stitch to the five remaining 2½" x 42" strips. Trim to 2½" x 50½" and stitch between each horizontal row of blocks and sashing.

4. Refer to Applique and Embroidery (steps 1, 2, & 5), Borders, and Layering and Finishing instructions to complete quilt. Instead of trimming the border strips to fit the quilt, you will be stitching strips together to adjust measurements to the top you completed in step 3.

Butterfly House

Butterfly House

MATERIALS NEEDED

Unpainted butterfly house
Acrylic craft paints: dark brown,
    yellow, dark green, light green,
    medium blue, ivory, charcoal,
    and lavender for house;
    colors of choice for butterflies
Assorted paint brushes
Crackle medium

Scotch Magic™ Tape
Ruler
Tracing paper
Graphite transfer paper
Matte spray varnish
Antiquing medium
Stencil - ¼" checkerboard

PAINTING THE HOUSE

Refer to the color photo on page 128 for guidance as needed.

1. Paint roof with one coat of dark brown acrylic paint. Dry thoroughly.

2. Following manufacturer's directions, apply crackle medium to painted roof. Dry thoroughly.

3. Apply a quick, even coat of yellow paint to roof. Crackles will appear in painted surface. Do not touch, as surface is very fragile when wet. Dry thoroughly.

4. Apply one coat of dark green paint to door. Allow to dry thoroughly, then repeat steps 2 and 3 to apply crackle medium and topcoat of light green paint.

5. Apply two coats of same light green paint to rest of house.

6. Use a ¼" checkerboard stencil to apply checks with the dark green paint.

7. Paint base of house medium blue.

8. Measure 1" up from base of house, and mark guidelines in pencil. Apply strip of Scotch Magic™ Tape along guideline on all four sides of house. Paint area below tape with ivory paint. Leave tape in place for now.

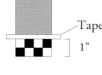

Tape

1"

Paint white

9. Measure and use ruler to mark two rows of ½" checks on ivory border. Paint every other check with charcoal paint in checkerboard fashion. Allow to dry throroughly and remove tape.

Tape

1"

10. Trace butterfly pattern below onto tracing paper. Position tracing paper on birdhouse front where you wish butterflies to appear. Tape in place, leaving one side open. Slide graphite paper under tracing paper, and use ballpoint pen to transfer design. Remove tape, tracing, and graphite paper.

11. Paint butterflies in colors of choice. Allow to dry thoroughly.

12. Apply a coat of matte spray varnish, and follow manufacturer's directions to apply antiquing medium to entire house. Finish with final coat of matte spray varnish.

Butterfly pattern

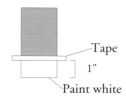

Blossoms & Butterflies Table Quilt

A wonderful whole-cloth, *patchwork print takes center stage in this soft-as-a-breeze springtime table topper. What could be faster, or more fuss-free?*

A striking butterfly *print frames it perfectly, while providing the source for the all-in-one machine stitched appliqués. Read all instructions before beginning, and use ¼"-wide seams throughout.*

Blossoms and Butterflies Table Quilt
Finished Size: 41½" square
Photo: page 131

FABRIC REQUIREMENTS

Center Panel - ⅝ yard
Inside Border - ⅛ yard
Corner Triangles - ½ yard
Accent Border - ¼ yard
Outside Border - 1 yard

Applique Butterfly Print - ¼ yard
Binding - ½ yard
Backing - 1⅜ yard *
Lightweight Batting - 46" square
*Fabric must measure 45" wide

CUTTING THE STRIPS AND PIECES

Read first paragraph of Cutting the Strips and Pieces on page 5.

		FIRST CUT		SECOND CUT	
		Number of Strips or pieces	Dimensions	Number of Pieces	Dimensions
	CENTER PANEL	1	17¼" square		
	INSIDE BORDER	2	1½" × 42"	2 2	1½" × 17¼" 1½" × 19¼"
	CORNER TRIANGLE	2	14¾" squares		
	ACCENT BORDER	4	1½" × 42"		
	OUTSIDE BORDER	4	6½" × 42"		
	BINDING	5	2¾" × 42"		

ASSEMBLY

1. Sew 1½" x 17¼" inside border strips to opposite sides of 17¼" center panel. Press toward border strips. Sew 1½" x 19¼" inside border strips to remaining sides. Press.

2. Cut 14¾" squares in half once diagonally to make two triangles. Sew one triangle to each side of unit from step 1. Press toward triangles. Square up quilt if necessary to measure 27" square.

3. Measure quilt through center from top to bottom. Cut two 1½" x 42" accent border strips to this measurement. Sew to sides. Press seams toward accent borders.

4. Measure quilt through center from side to side including borders. Cut remaining 1½" x 42" accent border strips to this measurement. Sew to top and bottom. Press.

5. Repeat steps 3 and 4 to fit, trim, and sew 6½"-wide outside borders to sides, top, and bottom of quilt. Press.

APPLIQUÉ

1. Referring to Quick-Fuse Appliqué directions on page 217, cut four butterfly motifs from butterfly print.

2. Refer to layout on page 130. Position and fuse one butterfly cut out in each corner triangle as shown.

3. Machine satin stitch or machine blanket stitch around butterflies.

LAYERING AND FINISHING

1. Layer backing, batting, and top together, referring to Layering the Quilt directions on page 217.

2. Machine or hand quilt as desired.

3. Cut one 2¾" x 42" binding strip into four equal pieces. Sew one piece to each remaining 2¾" x 42" strip. Refer to Binding the Quilt directions on page 217 to finish.

Summer

The good ol' summertime ... the flowers are bursting into bloom, the hot sunshine is smiling down upon us, and our feathered friends have nestled into their whimsical birdhouse homes to enjoy the summer season. And, of course, this inviting garden scene wouldn't be complete without those playful ladybugs adding their colorful charm.

Just sit back, relax, and bask in that warm, summertime glow. You'll have plenty of time to do just that ... and create touches of the season for your home, too, with our fast and easy projects.

Birdhouse Sampler Quilt

Birdhouse Sampler Quilt
Finished Size: 51" x 71"
Photo: page 139

This friendly

"neighborhood" adds a welcome touch to any room in your home! You'll have so much fun making this quilt, you'll want to use one or two of the patterns to make matching decorative pillows for your bed or favorite reading chair.

We've listed

instructions for each block separately, so you can mix and match to your heart's content. Read all instructions before beginning and use ¼"-wide seams throughout.

GENERAL FABRIC REQUIREMENTS

Fabrics for individual houses are listed with those blocks

Fabric A (Background) - ¾ yard of two different fabrics

Birdhouse Holes - Scraps

Block Frame - ⅝ yard

Corner Squares - ⅛ yard

Sashing and Inside Border - ¾ yard

Outside Border - ⅞ yard

Binding - ⅝ yard

Backing - 3⅛ yards

Lightweight Batting - 53" x 73" piece

134

GENERAL CUTTING THE STRIPS AND PIECES

Read first paragraph of Cutting the Strips and Pieces on page 5.

	FIRST CUT		SECOND CUT	
	Number of Strips	Dimensions	Number of Pieces	Dimensions
FABRIC A	See individual blocks			
BLOCK FRAME	12	1½" x 42"	24	1½" x 16½"
CORNER SQUARES	1	1½" x 42"	24	1½" square
SASHING	4	2½" x 42"	8	2½" x 18½"
INSIDE BORDER	5	2½" x 42"		
OUTSIDE BORDER	6	4½" x 42"		
BINDING	7	2¾" x 42"		

MAKING THE BLOCKS

Whenever possible, use the Assembly Line Method on page 5. Press in direction of arrows in diagrams.

BUNGALOW BIRDHOUSE BLOCK		Number of Pieces	Dimensions
	FABRIC REQUIREMENTS		FIRST CUT
FABRIC A (background)	1/8 yard	2	2½" x 9½"
		2	1½" x 6½"
		2	1½" x 6"
		2	1½" x 5½"
		2	1½" squares
FABRIC B (upper house)	1/8 yard	1	3½" x 2"
		4	1½" x 4"
		1	1½" x 12½"
		4	1½" squares
FABRIC C (windows)	scraps	2	3" x 4"
FABRIC D (window boxes)	scraps	2	1½" x 5"
FABRIC E (lower house & tower)	scraps	2	5" x 4"
		1	3½" x 2½"
FABRIC F (door)	scrap	1	3½" x 7"
FABRIC G (roof)	1/8 yard	1	3½" x 14½"
		2	1½" x 6"
		1	1½" x 4½"
FABRIC H (base)	1/8 yard	1	1½" x 16½"

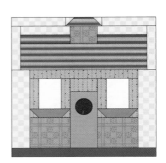

Bungalow Birdhouse Block
Block measures 16½" x 16½"

BLOCK ASSEMBLY

1. Sew each 3" x 4" Fabric C piece between two 1½" x 4" Fabric B pieces. Press. Make two.

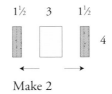

Make 2

2. Refer to Quick Corner Triangle directions on page 216. Sew two 1½" Fabric B squares to each 1½" x 5" Fabric D piece as shown. Press. Make two.

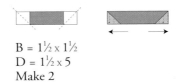

B = 1½ x 1½
D = 1½ x 5
Make 2

3. Sew each unit from step 2 between one unit from step 1 and one 5" x 4" Fabric E piece as shown. Press. Make two.

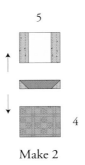

Make 2

4. Sew 3½" x 2" Fabric B piece to 3½" x 7" Fabric F piece as shown. Press.

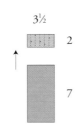

5. Sew unit from step 4 between two units from step 3. Press.

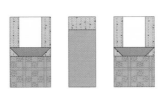

6. Sew 1½" x 12½" Fabric B piece to unit from step 5 as shown. Press.

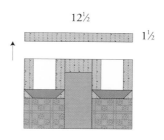

7. Sew unit from step 6 between two 2½" x 9½" Fabric A pieces. Press.

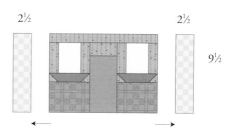

8. Sew 1½" x 6" Fabric A piece to each 1½" x 6" Fabric G piece.

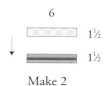

Make 2

9. Sew 3½" x 2½" Fabric E piece between units from step 8. Press.

10. Sew unit from step 9 to 3½" x 14½" Fabric G strip as shown. Press.

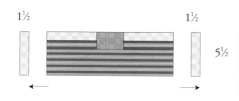

11. Sew unit from step 10 between two 1½" x 5½" Fabric A pieces. Press.

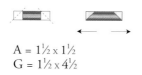

12. Refer to Quick Corner Triangle directions. Sew two 1½" Fabric A squares to 1½" x 4½" Fabric G piece as shown. Press.

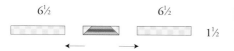

A = 1½ x 1½
G = 1½ x 4½

13. Sew unit from step 12 between two 1½" x 6½" Fabric A pieces. Press.

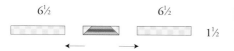

14. Sew unit from step 13 to unit from step 11 as shown. Press.

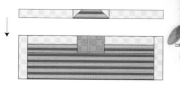

15. Refer to layout on page 136 and color photo on page 139. Sew unit from step 7 between unit from step 14 and 1½" x 16½" Fabric H strip. Press toward bottom edge of block.

16. Trace appliqué design from page 143. Make template and use scrap to cut one birdhouse hole #2. Cut out appliqué, adding ¼" seam allowance. Machine stitch or refer to Hand Appliqué directions on page 216 to appliqué birdhouse hole on door.

VINE STREET BIRDHOUSE BLOCK		Number of Pieces	Dimensions
	FABRIC REQUIREMENTS		**FIRST CUT**
FABRIC A (background)	⅓ yard	2 2 2	3½" x 8½" 3½" x 6½" 5½" squares
FABRIC B (pillars & upper roof appliqués)	scraps	2 2	1½" x 5½" 1¼" x 9"
FABRIC C (door)	scrap	1	2½" x 5½"
FABRIC D (lower house)	scraps	2 2	3½" x 6½" 1½" squares
FABRIC E (lower roof)	scrap	1	4½" x 1½"
FABRIC F (upper house)	¼ yard	1 2 1	6½" x 10½" 2" x 2½" 5½" x 2½"
FABRIC G (windows)	scraps	2	1½" x 2½"
FABRIC H (base)	⅛ yard	1	2½" x 16½"

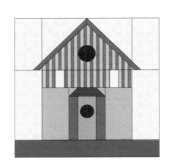

**Vine Street
Birdhouse Block**
Block measures 16½" x 16½"

BLOCK ASSEMBLY

1. Sew 2½" x 5½" Fabric C piece between two 1½" x 5½" Fabric B pieces. Press.

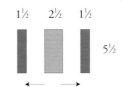

2. Refer to Quick Corner Triangle directions on page 216. Sew two 1½" Fabric D squares to 4½" x 1½" Fabric E piece as shown. Press.

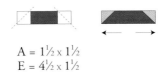

A = 1½ x 1½
E = 4½ x 1½

3. Sew unit from step 2 to unit from step 1 as shown. Press.

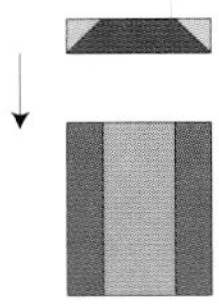

4. Sew unit from step 3 between two 3½" x 6½" Fabric D pieces. Press.

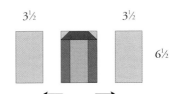

5. Arrange and sew two 2" x 2½" Fabric F pieces, two 1½" x2½" Fabric G pieces, and one 5½" x 2½" Fabric F piece in order shown to make a horizontal row. Press.

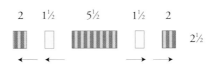

6. Sew unit from step 5 to unit from step 4. Press.

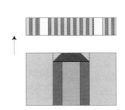

7. Sew unit from step 6 between two 3½" x 8½" Fabric A pieces. Press.

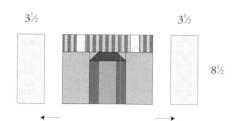

8. Refer to Quick Corner Triangle directions on page 110. Sew two 5½" Fabric A squares to 6½" x 10½" Fabric F piece as shown. Press.

A = 5½ x 5½
F = 6½ x 10½

9. Sew unit from step 8 between two 3½" x 6½" Fabric A pieces. Press.

10. Refer to layout on page 138 and color photo. Sew unit from step 7 between unit from step 9 and 2½" x 16½" Fabric H strip. Press toward bottom edge of block.

11. Trace appliqué designs from page 143. Make templates and use scraps to cut one each of birdhouse hole #1 and #2. Cut out appliqués, adding ¼" seam allowance.

12. Machine stitch or refer to Hand Appliqué directions on page 216. Appliqué two 1¼" x 9" Fabric B roof pieces over roof. Follow seam lines, and square ends as shown. Trace appliqué designs from page 143. Refer to layout on page 138 and color photo to appliqué birdhouse hole #2 on upper house, and birdhouse hole #1 on door.

PICKET FENCE BIRDHOUSE BLOCK		Number of Pieces	Dimensions
	FABRIC REQUIREMENTS		FIRST CUT
FABRIC A (background)	¼ yard	2 2 2	6½" squares 2½" x 6½" 3½" x 9½"
FABRIC B (fence)	⅛ yard	5 2	1½" x 3½" 1" x 10½"
FABRIC C (lower house)	¼ yard	1 1	5" x 10½" 1½" x 10½"
FABRIC D (house trim)	⅛ yard	1	1" x 10½"
FABRIC E (middle house)	⅛ yard	1	2½" x 10½"
FABRIC F (upper house)	¼ yard	2	6½" squares
FABRIC G (base)	⅛ yard	1	1½" x 16½"
ROOF APPLIQUÉS	⅛ yard	2	1¼" x 9"

Picket Fence Birdhouse Block
Block measures 16½" x 16½"

BLOCK ASSEMBLY

1. Fold 1½" x 3½" Fabric B piece in half lengthwise with right sides together. Using ¼" seam, stitch across top edge of each piece. Turn sewn pieces right side out. Press point at top, then turn under ¼" seam allowance on long sides and press. Make five.

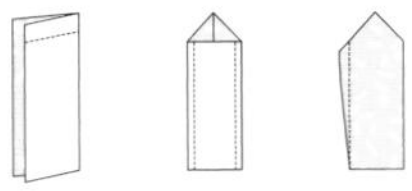

B = 1½ x 3½
Make 5

2. Sew 5" x 10½" Fabric C piece, one 1" x 10½" Fabric B piece, 1½"x 10½" Fabric C piece, and remaining 1" x 10½" Fabric B piece together as shown. Press.

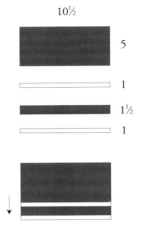

3. Refer to layout on this page and color photo on page 139. Machine stitch or refer to Hand Appliqué directions on page 216 to appliqué fence posts from step 1 to unit from step 2.

4. Sew 1" x 10½" Fabric D piece between 2½" x 10½" Fabric E piece and unit from step 3. Press.

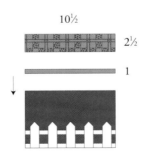

5. Sew unit from step 4 between two 3½" x 9½" Fabric A pieces. Press.

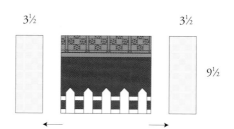

6. Refer to Quick Corner Triangle directions on page 216. Sew 6½" Fabric A and 6½" Fabric F squares together in pairs. Press. Make two.

A = 6½ x 6½
F = 6½ x 6½
Make 2

7. Arrange and sew two 2½" x 6½" Fabric A pieces and units from step 6 to make a horizontal row as shown. Press.

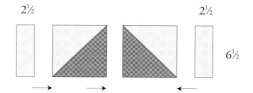

8. Refer to layout on page 140 and color photo on page 139. Sew unit from step 5 between unit from step 7, and 1½" x 16½" Fabric G strip. Press toward bottom edge of block.

9. Trace appliqué designs from page 143. Make templates and use scraps to cut one each of birdhouse hole #1 and #2. Cut out appliqués, adding ¼" seam allowance.

10. Machine stitch or refer to Hand Appliqué directions on page 216. Appliqué two 1¼" x 9" roof pieces over roof. Follow seam lines, and square ends as shown. Refer to layout on page 140 and color photo on page 139 to appliqué birdhouse holes on upper house and lower house as shown.

SUNSET BIRDHOUSE BLOCK		Number of Pieces	Dimensions
FABRIC REQUIREMENTS		FIRST CUT	
FABRIC A (background)	¼ yard	2 2 2 2	8½" squares 3½" squares 3" x 2" 2" x 6"
FABRIC B (lower house)	⅛ yard	1	3½" x 13½"
FABRIC C (upper house & trim #1)	¼ yard	1 1 1	8½" x 16½" 1½" x 13½" 1" x 13½"
FABRIC D (trim #2)	⅛ yard	1	1½" x 13½"
FABRIC E (birdhouse base & roof appliqués)	⅛ yard	1 2	2" x 11½" 1⅝" x 11¾"
FABRIC F (base #2)	⅛ yard	1	1½" x 16½"

Sunset
Birdhouse Block
Block measures 16½" x 16½"

BLOCK ASSEMBLY

1. Refer to Quick Corner Triangle directions on page 216. Sew two 3½" Fabric A squares to 3½" x 13½" Fabric B strip as shown. Press.

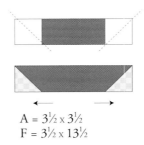

A = 3½ x 3½
F = 3½ x 13½

2. Arrange and sew 1½" x 13½" Fabric C strip, 1½" x 13½" Fabric D strip, 1" x 13½" Fabric C strip, and unit from step 1 to make a vertical row as shown. Press.

13½

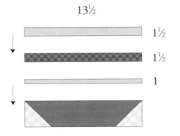

1½

1½

1

3. Sew unit from step 2 between two 2" x 6" Fabric A pieces. Press.

2   2

6

4. Refer to Quick Corner Triangle directions on page 216. Sew two 8½" Fabric A squares to 8½" x 16½" Fabric C strip as shown. Press.

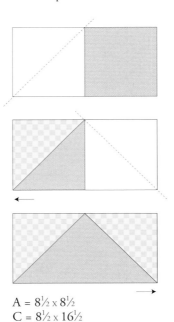

A = 8½ x 8½
C = 8½ x 16½

5. Sew 2" x 11½" Fabric E piece between two 3" x 2" Fabric A pieces as shown. Press.

6. Refer to layout on page 36 and color photo. Arrange and sew unit from step 4, unit from step 3, unit from step 5, and 1½" x 16½" Fabric F strip to make a vertical row. Press.

7. Trace appliqué designs. Make template and use scrap to cut one birdhouse hole #2. Cut out appliqué, adding ¼" seam allowance.

8. Machine stitch or refer to Hand Appliqué directions on page 216. Appliqué two 1⅝" x 11¾" Fabric E pieces over roof. Follow seam lines, and square ends as shown. Refer to layout on page 142 and color photo to appliqué birdhouse hole on upper house as shown.

Make finished size 1⅝"

#2

Birdhouse Holes
(only two sizes required
for entire quilt)

Make finished size 1¼"

#1

SCHOOLHOUSE BIRDHOUSE BLOCK		Number of Pieces	Dimensions
	FABRIC REQUIREMENTS		FIRST CUT
FABRIC A (background)	¼ yard	2 2 2	7½" square 1½" x 7½" 2½" x 7½"
FABRIC B (small gable)	scrap	1	4½" x 3½"
FABRIC C (large gable)	⅛ yard	2 1 2	5½" x 3½" 3½" x 14½" 2½" square
FABRIC D (schoolhouse trim)	⅛ yard	1	1½" x 14½"
FABRIC E (roof appliqués)	⅛ yard	2 2	1¼" x 10½" 1" x 4½"
FABRIC F (windows)	scraps	2	2½" x 4"
FABRIC G (schoolhouse front)	⅙ yard	4 4 1	2½" x 1½" 1¾" x 6" 3½" x 2"
FABRIC H (lower wall)	scrap	2	2" x 5"
FABRIC I (door)	scrap	1	3½" x 6"
FABRIC J (base)	⅛ yard	2 2	1½" x 7" 1½" x 6½"
FABRIC K (steps)	scraps	1 1	1½" x 3½" 1½" x 4½"

Schoolhouse Birdhouse Block
Block measures 16½" x 16½"

BLOCK ASSEMBLY

1. Refer to Quick Corner Triangle directions on page 216. Sew two 2½" Fabric C squares to 4½" x 3½" Fabric B piece as shown. Press.

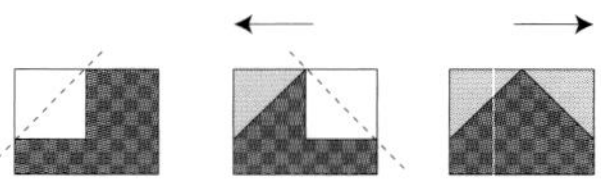

B = 4½ x 3½
C = 2½ x 2½

2. Sew unit from step 1 between two 5½" x 3½" Fabric C pieces. Press.

5½   5½

3½

3. Sew unit from step 2 between 3½" x 14½" Fabric C strip and 1½" x 14½" Fabric D strip. Press.

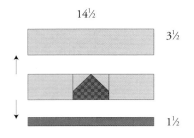

14½

3½

1½

4. Refer to Quick Corner Triangle directions on page 216. Sew two 7½" Fabric A squares to unit from step 3 as shown. Press.

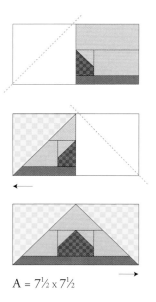

A = 7½ x 7½

5. Sew unit from step 4 between two 1½" x 7½" Fabric A pieces. Press.

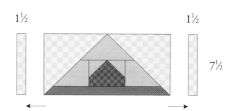

6. Sew two 2½" x 1½" Fabric G pieces to each 2½" x 4" Fabric F piece as shown. Press. Make two.

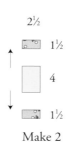

Make 2

7. Sew each unit from step 6 between two 1¾" x 6" Fabric G pieces as shown. Press. Make two.

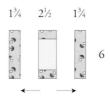

8. Sew one 2" x 5" Fabric H piece to each unit from step 7 as shown. Press. Make two.

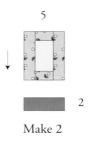

Make 2

9. Sew 3½" x 2" Fabric G piece to 3½" x 6" Fabric I piece as shown. Press.

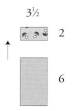

10. Arrange and sew two 2½" x 7½" Fabric A pieces, two units from step 8, and unit from step 9 to make a horizontal row as shown. Press.

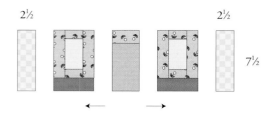

11. Sew 1½" x 3½" Fabric K piece between two 1½" x 7" Fabric J pieces. Label this Row A, and press. Repeat to sew 1½" x 4½" Fabric K piece between two 1½" x 6½" Fabric J pieces. Label this Row B, and press.

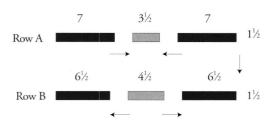

12. Refer to layout on page 144 and color photo on page 139. Arrange and sew unit from step 5, unit from step 10, and rows A and B from step 11. Press toward bottom edge of block.

13. Trace appliqué designs from page 143. Make templates and use scraps to cut one each of birdhouse hole #1 and #2. Cut out appliqués, adding ¼" seam allowance.

14. Refer to layout on page 144 and color photo on page 139. Machine stitch or refer to Hand Appliqué directions on page 216. Appliqué two 1¼" x 10½" Fabric E roof pieces over large gable and two 1" x 4½" Fabric E roof pieces over small gable. Follow seam lines, and square ends as shown. Appliqué birdhouse hole #1 to small gable and birdhouse hole #2 to door.

THREE'S COMPANY BIRDHOUSE BLOCK		Number of Pieces	Dimensions
	FABRIC REQUIREMENTS		FIRST CUT
FABRIC A (background)	⅙ yard	2 2 4	2" x 8" 2" squares 4½" squares
FABRIC B (lower house)	¼ yard	1 1 2	13½" x 5" 13½" x 2½" 2½" x 1½"
FABRIC C (perch & roof appliqués)	⅛ yard	1 2 2 2	1½" x 9½" 1¼" x 6½" 1¼" x 4½" 1¼" x 2½"
FABRIC D (upper house)	¼ yard	1 2	8½" x 6" 4½" x 2"
FABRIC E (birdhouse base #1)	⅛ yard	1	1½" x 16½"
FABRIC F (birdhouse base #2)	⅛ yard	1	2½" x 16½"
STAR APPLIQUÉ	scrap	1	5" square

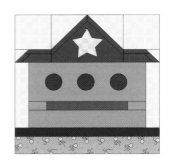

Three's Company Birdhouse Block

Block measures 16½" x 16½"

BLOCK ASSEMBLY

1. Sew 1½" x 9½" Fabric C piece between two 2½" x 1½" Fabric B pieces as shown. Press.

2½"   9½"   2½"

1½"

2. Sew unit from step 1 between 13½" x 5" Fabric B strip and 13½" x 2½" Fabric B strip. Press.

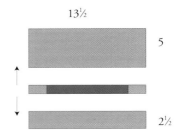

13½

5

2½

3. Sew unit from step 2 between two 2" x 8" Fabric A pieces. Press.

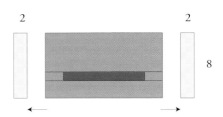

2   2

8

4. Refer to Quick Corner Triangle directions on page 216. Sew two 4½" Fabric A squares to 8½" x 6" Fabric D piece as shown. Press.

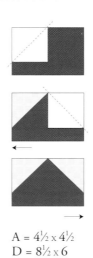

A = 4½ x 4½
D = 8½ x 6

5. Refer to Quick Corner Triangle directions on page 216. Sew one 2" Fabric A square to each 4½" x 2" Fabric D piece as shown. Press. Make one of each.

A = 2 x 2
D = 4½ x 2
Make 1 of each

6. Sew remaining 4½" Fabric A squares to each unit from step 5 as shown. Press. Make one of each.

4½

4½

Make 1 of each

7. Sew unit from step 4 between units from step 6 as shown. Press.

8. Refer to layout on page 146 and color photo on page 139. Arrange and sew unit from step 7, unit from step 3, 1½" x 16½" Fabric E strip, and 2¼" x 16½" Fabric F strip to make a vertical row. Press toward bottom edge of block.

9. Trace appliqué designs from page 143 and below. Make templates and use scraps to cut one star and three of birdhouse hole #2. Cut out appliqués, adding ¼" seam allowance.

10. Refer to layout on page 146 and color photo on page 139. Machine stitch or refer to Hand Appliqué directions on page 216. Appliqué two 1¼" x 6½", two 1¼" x 4½", and two 1¼" x 2½" Fabric C roof pieces over roof line. Follow seam lines, and square ends as shown. Appliqué three of birdhouse hole #2 to lower house, and star to upper house.

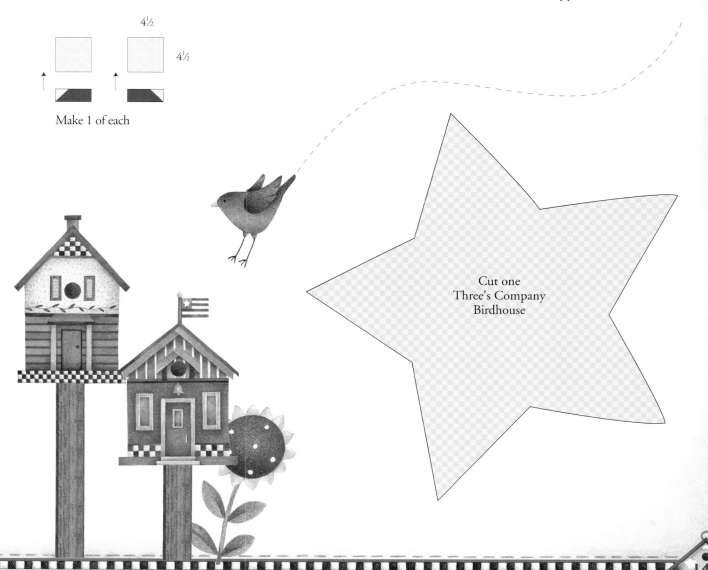

Cut one
Three's Company
Birdhouse

BIRDHOUSE SAMPLER QUILT ASSEMBLY

1. Sew 1½" x 16½" framing strips to top and bottom of each birdhouse block. Press toward framing strips.

2. Sew each remaining 1½" x 16½" framing strip between two 1½" corner squares. Press toward framing strips.

3. Sew unit from step 2 to sides of each birdhouse block. Press away from block.

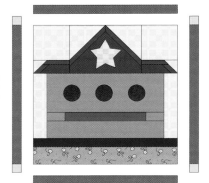

Corner square = 1½ x 1½
Frame = 1½ x 16½

4. Refer to layout on page 134 and color photo on page 139. Arrange three birdhouse blocks and four 2½" x 18½" sashing strips in a vertical row. Sew, then press toward sashing strips. Make two rows.

5. Sew 2½" x 42" sashing strips together in pairs. Measure quilt through center from top to bottom, and trim sewn strips to this measurement.

6. Refer to layout on page 134 and color photo on page 139. Arrange the two birdhouse rows from step 1 and the three sashing strips from step 5, alternating them. Sew sashing and rows together. Press toward sashing strips.

7. Sew 4½" x 42" border strips end to end to make one continuous 4½"-wide strip. Measure quilt through center from side to side. Trim two 4½"-wide border strips to this measurement. Sew to top and bottom. Press toward border strips.

8. Measure quilt through center from top to bottom including borders just added. Trim two 4½"-wide strips to this measurement. Sew to sides and press.

LAYERING AND FINISHING

1. Cut backing crosswise into two equal pieces. Sew pieces together on the long edges to make one 56" x 84" (approximate) backing piece. Arrange and baste backing, batting, and top together referring to Layering the Quilt directions on page 217.

2. Hand or machine quilt as desired.

3. Cut one 2¾" x 42" binding strip in half and sew halves to two remaining 2¾" x 42" strips. Sew remaining 2¾" x 42" binding strips together in pairs. Using shorter strips for top and bottom and longer strips for sides, refer to Binding the Quilt directions on page 217 to finish.

Sunset Birdhouse Table Runner

Bring the tender glow of a summertime sunset to your table with this quick and easy table runner.

Finished size will be 17" x 63".

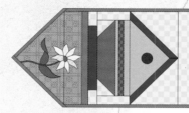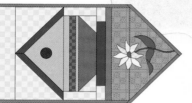

FABRIC REQUIREMENTS

Sunset Birdhouse Block - see fabric requirements page 142.
Triangle/ends - ⅜ yard cut into
　Two 3½" x 16½" pieces
　One 12¼" square cut once
　　diagonally

Background - ¼ yard cut into
　One 7½" x 16½" piece
Binding - ⅜ yard cut into
　Four 2¾" x 42" pieces
Backing - 1 yard

ASSEMBLY

1. Construct two Sunset Birdhouse Blocks following instructions beginning on page 142. Option: Make several table runners using different Sampler Birdhouse blocks for different rooms of your house.

2. Sew 7½" x 16½" background fabric between two Sunset Birdhouse Blocks.

3. Sew unit from step 2 between two 3½" x 16½" end pieces.

4. Cut 12¼" square once diagonally and sew triangles to the end pieces.

5. Quick fuse or hand appliqué flowers onto end pieces. Flower templates are found on page 155 in Chapel Birdhouse Wallhanging.

LAYERING AND FINISHING

1. Cut backing fabric lengthwise into two equal pieces. Sew pieces together to make one 22" x 72" (approximately) backing piece. Arrange and baste backing, batting, and top together, referring to Layering the Quilt directions on page 217.

2. Hand or machine quilt as desired. Trim batting ¼" from raw edge of table runner.

3. Sew 2¾" binding strips together end to end to make one continuous 2¾" strip. From this strip cut two 48" strips, and four 14" strips.

4. Sew binding following instructions on pages 188 and 189 for Falling Leaves Table Runner, Layering and Finishing steps 3 through 6.

Garden Chapel Wallhanging

Garden Chapel Wallhanging
Finished Quilt Size: 23" x 39"
Photo: page 153

June is the *month for weddings, and what summertime (or anytime) bride wouldn't be thrilled with this feminine, fanciful, flower-bedecked wallhanging?*

How about using *it to decorate at the wedding shower or reception, then present it afterward to the happy couple? No wedding on the horizon? It will be perfect at a garden party or afternoon tea, too. Read all instructions before beginning and use ¼"-wide seams throughout.*

FABRIC REQUIREMENTS

Fabric A (Door) - Scrap
Fabric B (Hedges) - Scraps
Fabric C (Center Wall) - ⅙ yard
Fabric D (Outside Walls) - ⅛ yard
Fabric E (Trim #1) - Scraps
Fabric F (Trim #2) - Scraps
Fabric G (Background) - ½ yard
Fabric H (House Base, Inside, and
   Outside Borders) - ⅓ yard
Fabric I (Post) - ⅛ yard
Fabric J (Upper Wall)-Scrap

Corners - Scraps
Middle Border - ¼ yard
Roof and Birdhouse Hole
   Appliqués - Scraps
Flower, Stem, and Leaf Appliqués -
   Assorted red, yellow, and
   green scraps
Binding - ⅜ yard
Backing - 1¼ yards
Lightweight Batting - 27" x 43" piece

150

CUTTING THE STRIPS AND PIECES

Read first paragraph of Cutting the Strips and Pieces on page 5.

		FIRST CUT		SECOND CUT	
		Number of Strips or Pieces	Dimensions	Number of Pieces	Dimensions
	FABRIC A	1	2½" x 7½"		
	FABRIC B	2	1" x 7½"		
	FABRIC C	1 1 1	6½" x 2½" 2" x 42" 1½" x 3½"	 2 2	 2" squares 2" x 6½"
	FABRIC D	2 2	2½" x 6½" 3½" squares		
	FABRIC E	2	1" x 4"		
	FABRIC F	2 1	2" x 4" 1" x 6½"		
	FABRIC G	1 2 2 2 2	6½" x 42" 4½" x 3½" 3½" squares 2½" x 8½" 1½" squares	1 2 2	6½" x 1½" 6½" x 12½" 4½" x 6½"
	FABRIC H	6	1½" x 42"	2 2 2 2 1	1½" x 36½" 1½" x 30½" 1½" x 20½" 1½" x 14½" 1½" x 12½"
	FABRIC I	1	2½" x 12½"		
	FABRIC J	1	6½" x 6"		
	CORNERS	8	1½" squares		
	MIDDLE BORDER	3	2½" x 42"	2 2	2½" x 16½" 2½" x 36½"
	ROOF APPLIQUÉS	1	1" x 42"	2 2 2	1" x 6" 1" x 4½" 1" x 3"
	BINDING	4	2¾" x 42"		

MAKING THE CENTER PANEL

For the center panel, you'll be making one birdhouse block, complete with base, post, and appliquéd flowers. Whenever possible, use the Assembly Line Method on page 5. Press in direction of arrows.

1. Sew 2½" x 7½" Fabric A piece between two 1" x 7½" Fabric B pieces. Press.

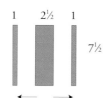

2. Refer to Quick Corner Triangle directions on page 216. Sew 2" Fabric C squares to unit from step 1 as shown. Press.

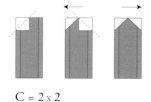

C = 2 x 2

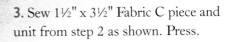

3. Sew 1½" x 3½" Fabric C piece and unit from step 2 as shown. Press.

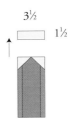
3½
1½

4. Sew one 2" x 6½" Fabric C piece to each 2½" x 6½" Fabric D piece as shown. Press. Make two.

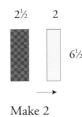
2½   2
6½

Make 2

5. Sew one 1" x 4" Fabric E piece to each 2" x 4" Fabric F piece as shown. Press. Make two.

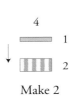
4
1
2

Make 2

6. Sew one unit from step 5 to each unit from step 4 as shown. Press.

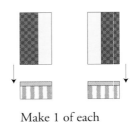

Make 1 of each

7. Arrange and sew two 2½" x 8½" Fabric G pieces, both units from step 6, and unit from step 3 in order shown to make a horizontal row. Press.

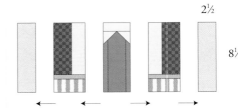
2½
8½

8. Refer to Quick Corner Triangle directions on page 216. Sew 3½" Fabric G squares to 6½" x 6" Fabric J piece as shown. Press.

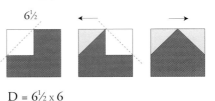
6½
6

D = 6½ x 6
G = 3½ x 3½

9. Arrange and sew 6½" x 1½" Fabric G piece, unit from step 8, 1" x 6½" Fabric F piece, and 6½" x 2½" Fabric C piece in order shown to make a vertical row. Press.

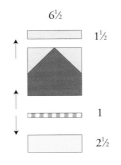
6½
1½
1
2½

10. Refer to Quick Corner Triangle directions on page 216. Sew one 3½" Fabric D square to each 4½" x 3½" Fabric G piece as shown. Press. Make one of each.

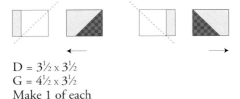

D = 3½ x 3½
G = 4½ x 3½
Make 1 of each

11. Sew one 4½" x 6½" Fabric G piece to each unit from step 10 as shown. Press. Make one of each.

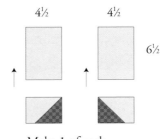
4½   4½
6½

Make 1 of each

12. Sew unit from step 9 between units from step 11 as shown. Press.

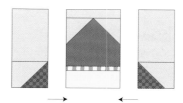

13. Sew unit from step 12 to unit from step 7 as shown. Press.

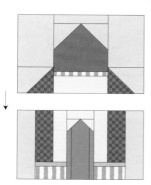

14. Sew 1½" x 12½" Fabric H piece between two 1½" Fabric G squares. Press.

15. Sew 2½" x 12½" Fabric I piece between two 6½" x 12½" Fabric G pieces. Press.

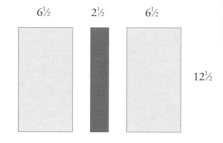

16. Refer to layout on page 150 and color photo on page 153. Arrange and sew units from steps 13, 14, and 15 in order shown to make a vertical row and complete center panel.

APPLIQUÉ

1. Trace appliqué designs. Make templates and use scraps to cut one upper and one lower birdhouse hole. Cut out appliqués, adding ¼" seam allowance.

2. Machine stitch or refer to Hand Appliqué on page 216. Appliqué upper birdhouse hole to birdhouse gable, and lower birdhouse hole to birdhouse door. Appliqué two 1" x 6" roof pieces over gable, two 1" x 4½" roof pieces over secondary roof line, and two 1" x 3" roof pieces over door. Follow seam lines, and square ends as shown. Refer to layout on page 150 and color photo on page 153 for guidance as needed.

3. Trace flower appliqué designs. Make templates and use scraps to trace one each of pieces 1 through 24. Cut out appliqués, adding ¼" seam allowance around each piece.

4. Referring to layout on page 150, and color photo on page 153, position appliqués around birdhouse post. Use your preferred method to stitch appliqués in place.

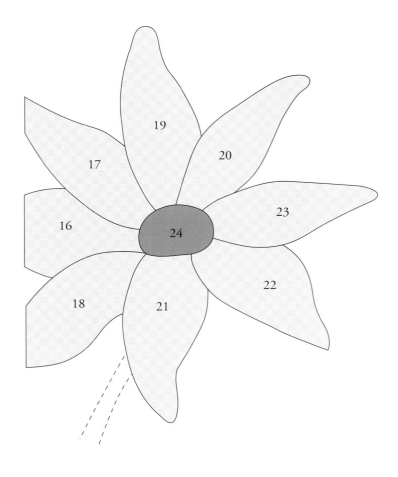

ASSEMBLY

1. Sew 1½" x 14½" Fabric H inside border strips to top and bottom of center panel. Press toward border strips.

2. Sew 1½" corner squares to short ends of each 1½" x 30½" Fabric H inside border strip. Press toward border strips. Sew strips to sides. Press.

3. Sew 2½" x 16½" middle border strips to top and bottom. Press toward middle borders.

4. Sew 2½" x 36½" middle border strips to sides. Press.

5. Sew 1½" x 20½" Fabric H outside border strips to top and bottom. Press.

6. Sew remaining 1½" corner squares to short ends of each 1½" x 36½" Fabric H outside border strip. Sew strips to sides. Press.

LAYERING AND FINISHING

1. Arrange and baste backing, batting, and top together referring to Layering the Quilt directions on page 217.

2. Hand or machine quilt as desired.

3. Refer to Binding the Quilt directions on page 217, and use 2¾" x 42" strips to finish.

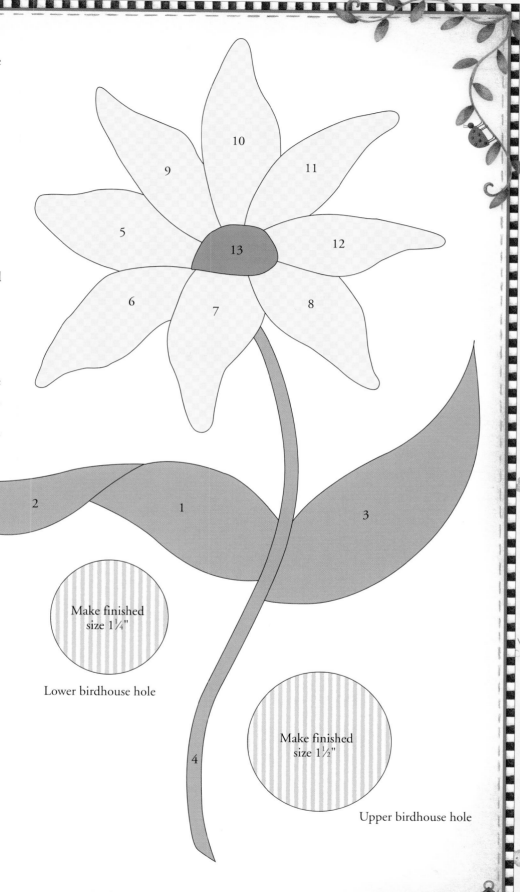

Make finished size 1¼"

Lower birdhouse hole

Make finished size 1½"

Upper birdhouse hole

Lots of Ladybugs Quilt

Lots of Ladybugs Quilt
Finished Quilt Size: 54" x 78" (not including prairie points)
Photo: page 159

Remember that
*favorite childhood chant—
"Ladybug, ladybug fly away home?"
It seems the ladybugs have come to
light on the summer-green leaves of
this delightful quilt.*

Black buttons and
*a touch of appliqué add whimsical
charm to the quick-pieced blocks, and
prairie point frame. Read all
instructions before beginning and
use ¼"-wide seams throughout.*

FABRIC REQUIREMENTS

Fabric A (Leaves and Stems) - ¾ yard
each of four different green fabrics
Fabric B (Ladybug Bodies) - ⅓ yard
each of four different red fabrics
Fabric C (Ladybug Heads) - Assorted
  black scraps
Fabric D (Background) - 2½ yards

Accent Border - ⅓ yard
Outside Border - ⅝ yard
Prairie Points - 1⅛ yards
Backing - 3½ yards
Lightweight Batting - 58" x 82" piece
192 assorted black buttons (⅜" - ¾")

CUTTING THE STRIPS AND PIECES

Read first paragraph of Cutting the Strips and Pieces on page 5.

		FIRST CUT		SECOND CUT	
		Number of Strips or Pieces	Dimensions	Number of Pieces	Dimensions
■	FABRIC A Repeat for each of four fabrics	4	4½" x 42"	30	4½" squares (leaves)
		2	2½" x 42"	24	2½" squares (leaves)
		1	1½" x 42"	12	1½" squares (leaves)
		1	1" x 42"	6	1" x 7" (stems)
■	FABRIC B Repeat for each of four fabrics	2	4½" x 42"	12	4½" squares
■	FABRIC C	48	1½" squares		
▦	FABRIC D	18	4½" x 42"	144	4½" squares
■	ACCENT BORDER	7	1½" x 42"		
▥	OUTSIDE BORDER	7	2½" x 42"		
■	PRAIRIE POINTS	9	4" x 42"	84	4" squares

MAKING THE BLOCKS

You will be making 24 leaf blocks. Each leaf block includes 2 ladybugs. The leaf block finishes 12" square. The "ladybug in the leaf" finishes 4" square.

Whenever possible, use the Assembly Line Method on page 5. Press in direction of arrows.

Ladybug Blocks

1. Refer to Quick Corner Triangle directions on page 216. For each block, sew two matching 2½" Fabric A squares to each 4½" Fabric B square. Press. Make forty-eight total.

Repeat to sew a matching 1½" Fabric A square and a scrappy 1½" Fabric C square to remaining two corners of each step 1 unit. Press.

B = 4½ x 4½
A = 2½ x 2½
Make 48

C = 1½ x 1½
A = 1½ x 1½

Leaf Blocks

1. Refer to Hand Appliqué directions on page 216. Hand or machine appliqué one 1" x 7" Fabric A piece diagonally over a 4½" Fabric D square as shown. Make twenty-four.

Make 24

2. Refer to Quick Corner Triangle directions on page 216. Sew 4½" Fabric A and Fabric D squares to make ninety-six units. Press.

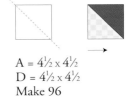

A = 4½ x 4½
D = 4½ x 4½
Make 96

3. Sew unit from step 2, a matching-color 4½" Fabric A square and a matching color appliquéd Fabric D square from step 1 in a row as shown. Press. Make twenty-four.

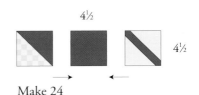

Make 24

4. Sew two matching ladybug blocks and a matching-color unit from step 2 in a row as shown. Press. Make twenty-four.

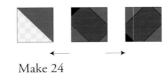

Make 24

5. Sew a remaining 4½" Fabric B square and two matching units from step 2 in a row as shown. Press. Make twenty-four.

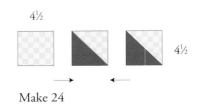

Make 24

6. Arrange matching-color rows from steps 3, 4, and 5 as shown. Sew the rows. Press.

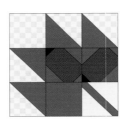

Make 24

ASSEMBLY

1. Refer to project layout on page 156 and color photo on page 159. Arrange blocks in a pleasing arrangement of six horizontal rows of four blocks each, rotating blocks as shown. Sew blocks into rows. Press seams in opposite directions from row to row.

2. Sew rows together. Press.

BORDERS

1. Cut one 1½" x 42" accent border strip in half and sew halves to two 1½" x 42" strips. Sew remaining 1½" x 42" accent border strips together in pairs. Repeat for outside border.

2. Sew 1½" accent borders to 2½" outside borders lengthwise. Press toward outside border.

3. Measure quilt through center vertically and horizontally.

4. Fold each border unit crosswise to find its midpoint and mark with a pin. Using quilt dimensions measured in step 3, measure each border unit from its midpoint and pin-mark border ends to show where edges of quilt will be.

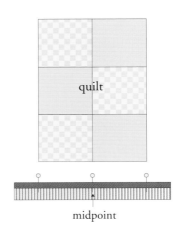

midpoint

7. Sew border to quilt, stopping and starting with a backstitch ¼" from pinmarked end points. Do not sew past pin marks at either end. Repeat to sew all four border units to quilt.

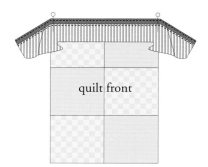

8. Fold one corner diagonally, right sides together, matching and pinning marked diagonal sewing lines. End points of adjacent seams should match.

Begin sewing with a backstitch at point where side seams ended. Sew to end of marked line at outside edge of strip. Trim excess border ¼" from seam and press open. Repeat on remaining corners. Press border seams to outside and mitered seams open.

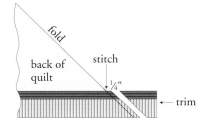

5. Beginning at a marked end point, draw a 45 degree diagonal line to represent mitered seam line. Repeat on opposite end of strip, drawing a mirror image diagonal line. Repeat for all four border units.

6. Align a border unit to quilt with accent border closest to quilt center. Pin at midpoints and pin-marked ends first, and then along entire side easing to fit if necessary.

LAYERING AND FINISHING

1. Use 4" squares to make 84 Prairie Points, folding each twice along the diagonal as shown.

Fold   Fold Again   Make 84

2. Starting at the center and working outwards, align and pin raw edges of 17 Prairie Points along top edge of quilt as shown, nesting one inside folds of another if necessary to adjust total width. Repeat on bottom edge of quilt.

Quilt Top

3. Pin 25 Prairie Points to each side of quilt in the same way. Triangle edges should meet at quilt corners.

4. Sew all Prairie Points to quilt with ¼" seams. Do not fold outwards.

5. Cut backing crosswise into two equal pieces. Sew together to make one 63" x 84" (approximate) backing piece. Arrange and baste backing, batting, and top together referring to Layering the Quilt directions on page 217.

6. Machine or hand quilt as desired. Leave 1" from all edges free from quilting.

7. Trim batting and backing to match quilt top, then trim an additional ¼" of batting from all sides.

8. Fold Prairie Points away from quilt, pointing them outward and seams under quilt top. Press. Turn under ¼" of backing and hand stitch in place, covering seams. Add more quilting around edges if desired.

9. Refer to layout on page 156 and color photo on page 159. Sew four small black buttons to each ladybug body as shown. (You may wish to vary the number of "spots").

Little Ladybug Wallhanging

Photo: page 132

Here's a smaller version of the Lots of Ladybugs Quilt. What a perfect way to celebrate the arrival of summer! Read all instructions before beginning and use ¼" seam allowances throughout. Finished size will be 30" square. (not including prairie points)

FABRIC REQUIREMENTS

Fabric A - (⅝ yard) or scraps
    Twenty 4½" squares (leaves)
    Sixteen 2½" squares (leaves)
    Eight 1½" squares (leaves)
    Four 1" x 7" strips (stems)

Fabric B (Ladybug Bodies) - scraps
    Eight 4½" squares

Fabric C (Ladybug Heads) - scraps
    Eight 1½" squares

Fabric D (Background) - ½ yard
    Three 4½" x 42" strips, cut into
    Twenty-four 4½" squares

Accent Border - ¼ yard
    Two 1½" x 24½" strips
    Two 1½" x 26½" strips

Outside Border - ⅓ yard
    Two 2½" x 26½" strips
    Two 2½" x 30½" strips

Prairie Points - ½ yard
    Four 4" x 42" strips, cut into
    Thirty-two 4" squares

Backing - 1 yard

Lightweight batting - 33" x 33" piece

Small Buttons - 32

MAKING THE BLOCKS

Refer to instructions in Lots of Ladybugs Quilt to make four leaf blocks. Each leaf block includes two ladybugs. The leaf block finishes 12" square. Stitch the four leaf blocks together and add borders.

BORDERS

1. Sew 1½" x 24½" accent border strips to top and bottom. Press toward border strips.

2. Sew 1½" x 26½" accent border strips to sides. Press.

3. Sew 2½" x 26½" outside border strips to top and bottom. Press.

4. Sew 2½" x 30½" outside border strips to sides. Press.

LAYERING AND FINISHING

1. Refer to Lots of Ladybugs Quilt and use 4" squares to make thirty-two Prairie Points.

161

Ladybug House

Our feathered friends *will fly away home to this loveable birdhouse. A whimsical ladybug welcomes them to this easy-to-paint haven.*

Crackle medium *and antiquing glaze give this painted project a vintage look. The same process can be used on flowerpots or furniture. You can have ladybugs everywhere!*

Ladybug House

MATERIALS NEEDED

Small, unpainted birdhouse
Acrylic craft paint: country red, ivory, black, and green for house and ladybug
Assorted paint brushes
Ruler

Two-step crackle medium
Tracing paper
Graphite transfer paper
Scotch Magic™ Tape
Matte spray varnish
Antiquing medium

PAINTING THE HOUSE

Refer to the color photo for guidance as needed.

1. Paint roof with two coats of country red acrylic paint. Allow to dry thoroughly.

2. Paint roof with ½" random black polka dots.

3. Paint roof edge ivory. Measure and use ruler to mark ¼" checks on ivory edge. Paint every other check with black paint.

4. Paint house ivory with two or three coats, until well covered.

5. Following manufacturer's directions for crackle medium, apply thick coat of part one to the walls of the house. Allow to dry thoroughly. Apply part two of crackle medium. Cracks are clear until house is antiqued.

6. Paint base of house and roof decoration with two coats of green paint. (On the sample shown, the roof decoration is a piece of dowel along the top edge of the roof.)

7. Trace ladybug pattern below onto tracing paper. Position tracing paper on birdhouse front where you wish ladybug to appear. Tape in place, leaving one side open. Slide graphite paper under tracing paper, and use ballpoint pen to transfer design. Remove tape, tracing, and graphite paper.

8. Refer to color photo and paint ladybug in colors of choice. Allow to dry thoroughly.

9. Apply a coat of matte spray varnish, and follow manufacturer's instructions to apply antiquing medium to entire house. Finish with final coat of matte spray varnish.

Ladybug pattern

Garden Stepping Stone

On a warm *summer day take a stroll down the garden path highlighted with the beauty of your flowers and the elegance of this glass mosaic stepping stone.*

Don't stop with *this project. Use other appliqués in this book to create mosaic birdhouse flowerpots, a birdhouse birdbath, or a garden bench. The possibilities are endless.*

Garden Stepping Stone

MATERIALS NEEDED

Fine-point felt-tip pen
Clear self-adhesive vinyl - 18" x 18"
16 " square concrete stepping stone
Assorted colors scrap glass
Ceramic tile adhesive
Tilers grout *
Sealant
Rags/sponge/wooden skewer stick
Safety glasses

*If less than ¼" space between glass
   use non-sanded grout, larger spaces
   between glass use a sanded grout.

PREPARING THE STEPPING STONE

1. Following diagram below, draw birdhouse design on the clear non-stick side of the self-adhesive vinyl. (DO NOT DRAW ON PAPER SIDE)

2. Peel backing off of vinyl. Fold under outside edges approximately ½" to itself to form a non-stick edge.

3. Wearing safety glasses and using glass mosaic cutting pliers, break glass into irregular shapes.

4. Place glass right side down onto sticky side of vinyl in a pleasing pattern.

5. Leave a minimum of $\frac{1}{16}$" to $\frac{1}{8}$" space between each piece of glass.

MAKING BIRDHOUSE STEPPING STONE

1. Apply ceramic tile adhesive to the clean surface of 16" concrete stone.

2. Carefully lift the vinyl with glass adhering to it, and place glass onto adhesive area.

3. Slowly peel away vinyl leaving glass on tile adhesive. Clean excess adhesive between glass with stick.

4. Let adhesive dry a minimum of 24 hours.

5. Following manufacturer's instructions, mix, and apply finish grout.

6. Apply sealant following product directions.

Mosaic Ideas

Decorate terra cotta pots and planters with the small birdhouse appliqués found in the Garden Tool Caddy section.

Decorate wooden frames.

Broken dishes? Don't despair, use in place of colored glass to create a mosaic piece.

Continue your outside theme by making mosaic pieces for the inside of your home.

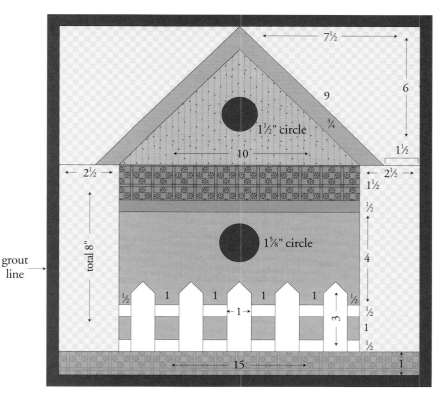

Stepping Stone layout

Garden Tool Caddy

Bring a touch *of whimsy to your gardening chores with this clever—and handy—embellished tote.*

Garden Tool Caddy

A purchased *organizer, personalized with your choice of quick-fuse appliqués, makes the perfect catch-all for gardening gloves, tools, and seed packets.*

Read all instructions before beginning, and use ¼"-wide seams throughout.

MATERIALS AND FABRIC NEEDED

Pocket bucket organizer - Comes in various colors and various pocket layouts.

Assorted scraps to coordinate with organizer colors for birdhouse appliqués

Accent Trim - See Assembly directions on page 167.

Binding - See Assembly directions on page 167.

Heavy duty fusible web - ⅛ yard

Bucket

ASSEMBLY

1. Remove purchased binding from organizer. Set it aside for now.

2. Measure width of organizer from raw edge to raw edge along its top edge. Cut one 2¼"-wide strip to that measurement from the accent trim fabric.

3. Turn under ¼"-wide seam allowance along long raw edges of 2¼"-wide accent trim strip, and press. Pin strip along top edge of organizer and topstitch in place by hand or machine.

Bucket

4. Refer to Quick-Fuse Appliqué directions on page 217. Trace one birdhouse appliqué design for each organizer pocket from patterns below. Center and quick-fuse designs to pockets, referring to color photo for placement.

5. Measure length of binding removed from organizer in step 1. Cut 2¾"-wide strips to equal that measurement, plus a little extra for seams and finishing. Attach binding, referring to Binding the Quilt directions on page 217.

Tool Caddy
Appliqués

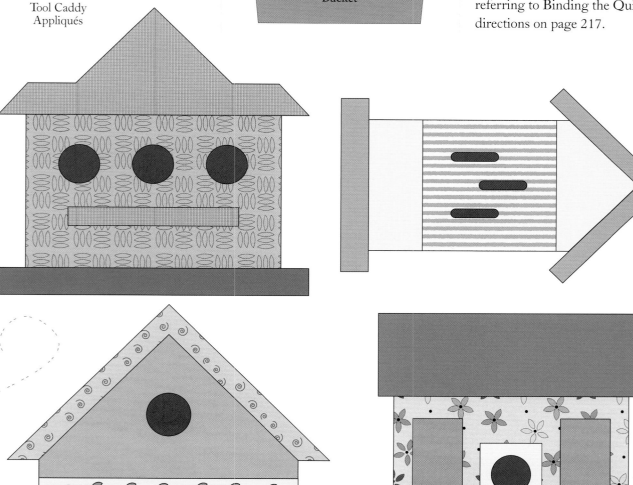

Autumn

It sneaks up on us every year. The leaves of gold and red begin to drift to the ground, and the harvest pumpkins are almost ripe on the vines. There's just a little chill in the afternoon air, and we know, once again, that glorious autumn has arrived.

Surrounded by the rich, vibrant colors of the season, the children head back to school, and our faithful friends begin to feather their nests or to think of their journeys south to find warmer homes. It's a great time to add cozy touches to your nest, too, with warm and wonderful projects created to celebrate the golden glow of autumn.

Fall Flight Quilt

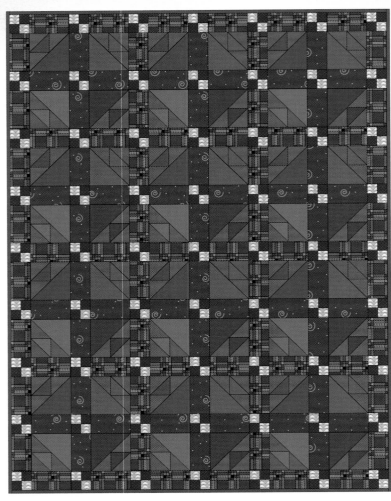

You'll welcome those first cool autumn nights as you snuggle under this cozy quilt! We've chosen a variety of warm browns for our soaring birds, winging south over a crisp blue sky.

Two-color sashing creates a charming effect, and snappy four-patch corner squares add pizzazz. Read all instructions before beginning and use 1/4" seams throughout.

Fall Flight Quilt
Finished Size: 58" x 76"
Photo: page 173

FABRIC REQUIREMENTS

Fabric A (Birds) - 1/4 yard *each* of eight different brown fabrics or fat quarters (18" x 22")

Fabric B (Background) - 1⅛ yards

Fabric C and D (Four Patches) ½ yard *each* of two contrasting fabrics

Inside Sashing - ⅞ yard

Outside Sashing - 1⅙ yards

Binding - ⅝ yard

Backing - 3⅝ yards

Lightweight Batting - 62" x 80"

CUTTING THE STRIPS AND PIECES

Read first paragraph of Cutting the Strips and Pieces on page 5.

	FIRST CUT		SECOND CUT	
	Number of Strips	Dimensions	Number of Pieces	Dimensions
FABRIC A Repeat for each of eight fabrics	1 1	6⅞" x 22" 3½" x 22"	3 6	6⅞" squares 3½" squares
FABRIC B	4 3	3½" x 42" 3⅞" x 42"	48 48	3½" squares 3⅞" squares
FABRIC C AND D Repeat for each fabric	7	2" x 42"		
INSIDE SASHING	8	3½" x 42"	48	3½" x 6½"
OUTSIDE SASHING	11	3½" x 42"	62	3½" x 6½"
BINDING	7	2¾" x 42"		

MAKING THE BLOCKS

You will be making forty-eight "bird" blocks and sixty-three four-patch corner squares. Whenever possible, use the Assembly Line Method on page 5. Press in direction of arrows in diagrams.

Bird Blocks

1. Refer to Quick Corner Triangle directions on page 216. Using 3½" Fabric A and Fabric B squares, make forty-eight units. Press.

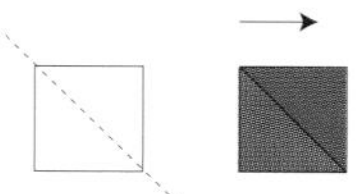

A = 3½ x 3½
B = 3½ x 3½
Make 48

2. Cut 3⅞" Fabric B squares in half once diagonally to make ninety-six triangles. Sew triangles to adjacent sides of each unit from step 1. Press.

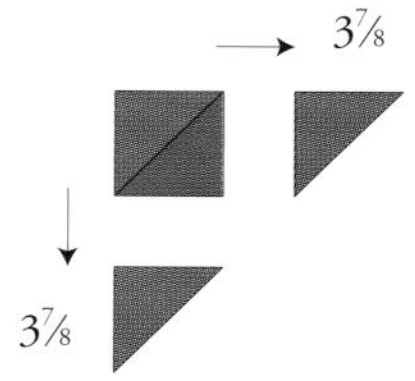

Make 48

3. Cut each 6⅞" Fabric A triangle in half once diagonally to make forty-eight triangles. Sew each triangle to a matching-color unit from step 2 as shown. Press. Block measures 6½" x 6½".

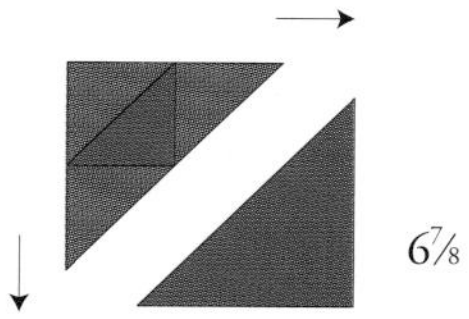

Make 48

Four-Patch Corner Squares

1. Sew 2" x 42" Fabric C and Fabric D strips together in pairs to make seven identical strip sets. Press toward darker fabric. Cut one hundred twenty-six 2" segments.

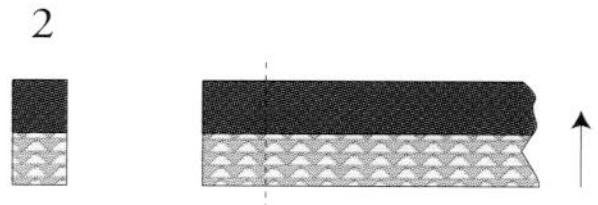

Cut 126 Make 7 strip sets

2. Sew segments from step 1 together in pairs. Press. Make sixty-three.

Make 63

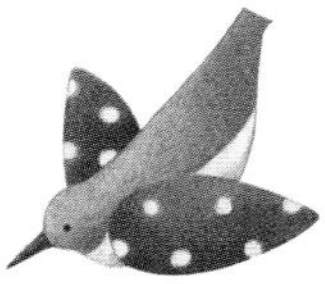

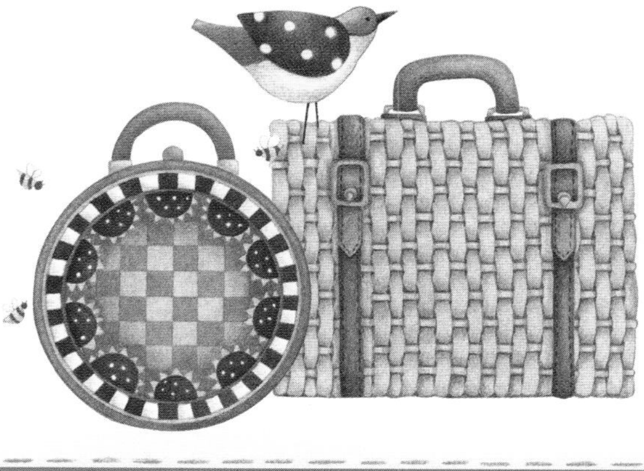

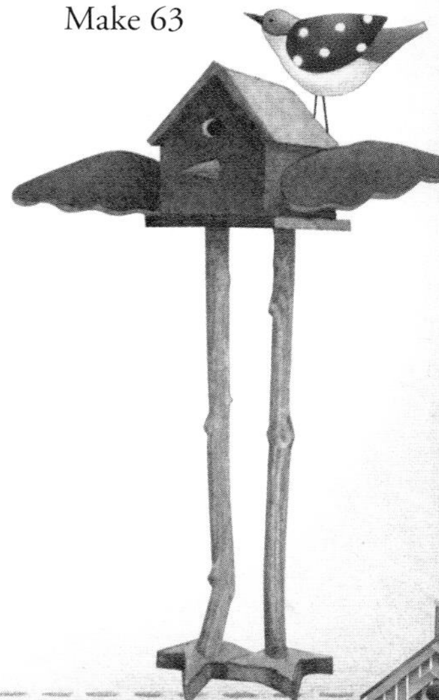

ASSEMBLY

1. Lay out six bird blocks, three 3½" x 6½" inside sashing pieces, and four 3½" x 6½" outside sashing pieces to make a horizontal row as shown. Sew blocks and strips together. Press seams toward sashing strips. Make eight rows.

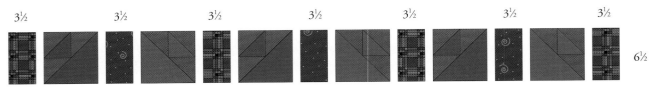

Make 8 Rows

2. Alternate seven pieced corner squares and six 6½" x 3½" outside sashing pieces to make a horizontal row as shown. Sew squares and strips together. Press seams toward sashing strips. Make five rows.

Make 5 Rows

3. Repeat step 2, substituting the 6½" x 3½" inside sashing strips for the outside sashing strips. Make four rows.

Make 4 Rows

4. Referring to layout on page 170 and color photo, lay out rows from steps 1 through 3 as shown. Join rows and press.

LAYERING AND FINISHING

1. Cut backing fabric crosswise into two equal pieces. Sew pieces together to make one 65" x 84" (approximate) backing piece. Arrange and baste backing, batting, and top together, referring to Layering the Quilt directions on page 217.

2. Machine or hand quilt as desired.

3. Cut one 2 ¾" x 42" binding strip in half and sew halves to two 2 ¾" x 42" strips. Sew remaining 2 ¾" x 42" binding strips in pairs. Using shorter strips for top and bottom and longer strips for sides, refer to Binding the Quilt directions on page 217 to finish.

Back -to- School Birdhouse

No matter how *grown up we get, we never seem to forget the excitement of back-to-school days. Revisit those wonderful times while stitching on this nostalgic schoolhouse.*

A log-cabin *printed fabric adds interest to the border without taking a lot of time. Read all instructions before beginning and use ¼"-wide seam allowances throughout.*

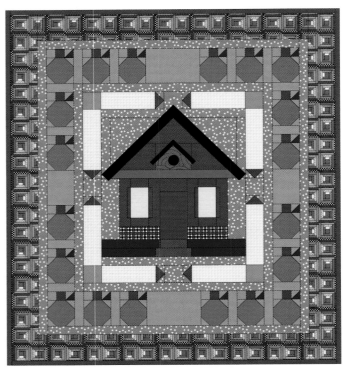

Back to School Birdhouse
Finished Quilt Size: 37" x 41"
Photo: page 178

FABRIC REQUIREMENTS

Fabric A (Small Gable) - Scraps
Fabric B (Large Gable) - ⅛ yard*
Fabric C (Schoolhouse Trim) - ⅛ yard
Fabric D (Schoolhouse and Pencil
    Background, Inside and Middle
    Borders) - ⅔ yard
Fabric E (Roof Appliqués and
    Birdhouse Hole) - ⅛ yard
Fabric F (Windows) - Scraps
Fabric G (Schoolhouse Front)
    ⅙ yard*
Fabric H (Lower Wall) - Scraps
Fabric I (Door and Shutters) - Scraps
Fabric J (Grass) - ⅛ yard
Fabric K (Steps) - Scraps
Fabric L (Pencils) - ⅙ yard

Fabric M (Pencil Points) - Scraps
Fabric N (Erasers) - Scraps
Fabric O (Apples) - ¼ yard (total)
    assorted red scraps**
Fabric P (Background and Sashing
    for Apple Blocks) - ½ yard
Fabric Q (Leaves) - Scraps
Fabric R (Apple Stems) - Scraps
Outside Border - ½ yard
Binding - ⅜ yard
Backing - 1⅙ yards
Lightweight Batting - 41" x 45" piece
    * We used ¼ yard (total) of the same
    fabric for the large gable and
    schoolhouse front. (Fabric G)
    ** We used five different red fabrics.

CUTTING THE STRIPS AND PIECES

Read first paragraph of Cutting the Strips and Pieces on page 5.

		FIRST CUT		SECOND CUT	
		Number of Strips or Pieces	Dimensions	Number of Pieces	Dimensions
	FABRIC A	1	4½" x 3½"		
	FABRIC B	1	3½" x 42"	2	3½" x 5½"
				1	3½" x 14½"
				2	2½" squares
	FABRIC C	1	1½" x 14½"		
	FABRIC D	2	7½" squares		
		5	1½" x 42"	2	1½" x 7½"
				16	1½" squares
				2	1½" x 16½"
				2	1½" x 20½"
				2	1½" x 24½"
		1	2½" x 42"	2	2½" x 7½"
				4	2½" squares
	FABRIC E	1	1½" x 42"	2	1½" x 12"
				2	1" x 4"
				1	2¼" square
	FABRIC F	2	2½" x 4"		
	FABRIC G	1	1½" x 42"	4	1½" x 2½"
		1	1¾" x 42"	4	1¾" x 6"
		1	2" x 3½"		
	FABRIC H	2	5" x 2"		
	FABRIC I	1	3½" x 6" (door)		
		4	1" x 4" (shutters)		
	FABRIC J	1	1½" x 42"	2	1½" x 7"
				2	1½" x 6½"
	FABRIC K	1	1½" x 3½"		
		1	1½" x 4½"		
	FABRIC L	2	2½" x 42"	4	2½" x 6½"
				4	2½" x 7½"
	FABRIC M	1	1½" x 42"	8	1½" x 2½"
	FABRIC N	4	2½" squares		
	FABRIC O	20	3½" squares		
	FABRIC P	6	1½" x 42"	120	1½" squares
				8	1½" x 3½"
		1	4½" x 42"	2	4½" x 6½"
				2	4½" x 3½"
				8	4½" x 1½"
	FABRIC Q	20	1½" squares		
	FABRIC R	20	1½" squares		

MAKING THE BLOCKS

In addition to the center schoolhouse block, you will be making eight pencils (four each in two different sizes) and twenty apple blocks. Whenever possible, use the Assembly Line Method, page 5. Press in direction of arrows.

Schoolhouse Block

1. Refer to Quick Corner Triangle directions on page 216. Sew 2½" Fabric B squares to 4½" x 3½" Fabric A piece as shown. Press.

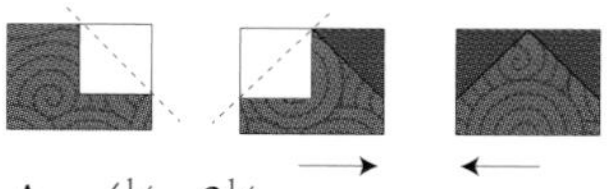

A = 4½ x 3½
B = 2½ x 2½

2. Sew unit from step 1 between two 3½" x 5½" Fabric B pieces. Press.

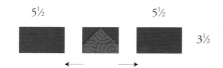

3. Sew unit from step 2 between 3½" x 14½" Fabric B strip and 1½" x 14½" Fabric C strip. Press.

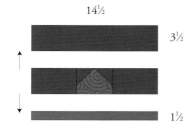

4. Refer to Quick Corner Triangle directions on page 216. Sew two 7½" Fabric D squares to unit from step 3 as shown. Press.

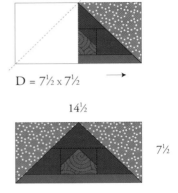

D = 7½ x 7½

D = 7½ x 7½

14½

7½

5. Sew unit from step 4 between two 1½" x 7½" Fabric D pieces. Press.

6. Sew 1½" x 2½" Fabric G pieces to each 2½" x 4" Fabric F piece as shown. Press. Make two.

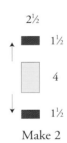

2½

1½

4

1½

Make 2

7. Sew each unit from step 6 between two 1¾" x 6" Fabric G pieces. Press. Make two.

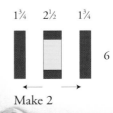

1¾   2½   1¾

6

Make 2

8. Sew one 5" x 2" Fabric H piece to each unit from step 7 as shown. Press. Make two.

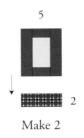

5

2

Make 2

9. Sew 2" x 3½" Fabric G piece to 3½" x 6" Fabric I piece as shown. Press.

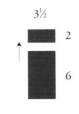

3½

2

6

10. Arrange and sew two 2½" x 7½" Fabric D pieces, two units from step 8, and unit from step 9 as shown. Press.

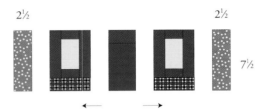

2½   2½

7½

11. Sew 1½" x 3½" Fabric K piece between two 1½" x 7" Fabric J pieces. Label this Row A, and press. Repeat to sew 1½" x 4½" Fabric K piece between two 1½" x 6½" Fabric J pieces. Label this Row B, and press.

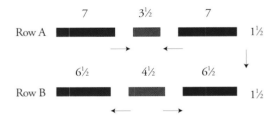

Row A   7   3½   7   1½

Row B   6½   4½   6½   1½

12. Refer to layout on page 174 and color photo on page 178. Arrange and sew unit from step 5, unit from step 10, and rows A and B from step 11 as shown. Press. Block will measure 16½".

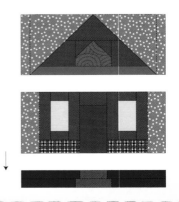

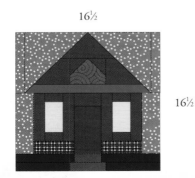

16½

16½

MAKING AND ADDING PENCIL BLOCKS

1. Refer to Quick Corner Triangle directions on page 110. Sew two 1½" Fabric D squares to each 1½" x 2½" Fabric M piece as shown. Press. Make eight.

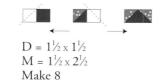

D = 1½ x 1½
M = 1½ x 2½
Make 8

2. Arrange and sew two units from step 1, one 2½" Fabric D square, and two 2½" x 6½" Fabric L pieces as shown. Press. Make two.

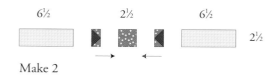

6½   2½   6½

2½

Make 2

3. Sew one 1½" x 16½" Fabric D strip to each unit from step 2. Press seams toward strip. Make two.

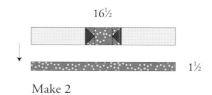

16½

1½

Make 2

4. Refer to layout on page 174 and color photo on page 178. Sew one unit from step 3 to top and bottom of schoolhouse block, positioning Fabric D strip closest to center block. Press seams toward strip.

5. Sew two remaining units from step 1, one 2½" Fabric D square, two 2½" x 7½" Fabric L pieces, and two 2½" Fabric N squares as shown. Press. Make two.

2½   7½   2½   7½   2½

2½

Make 2

6. Sew units from step 5 to sides of quilt. Press seams toward center block.

7. Sew 1½" x 20½" Fabric D inside border strips to top and bottom of quilt. Press seams toward border strips. Sew 1½" x 24½" inside border strips to sides. Press.

8. Trace appliqué design from page 143. Make template and cut one birdhouse hole #1 from Fabric E, adding ¼" seam allowance. Machine stitch or refer to Hand Appliqué on page 216. Appliqué two 1½" x 12" Fabric E roof pieces over large gable and two 1" x 4" Fabric E roof pieces over small gable. Follow seam lines, extending and squaring ends as shown. Appliqué one 1" x 4" Fabric I shutter piece on opposite sides of each window, and the birdhouse hole on the small gable.

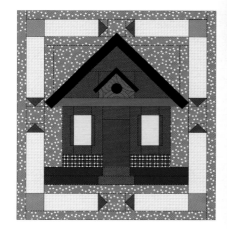

MAKING AND ADDING APPLE BLOCKS

1. Refer to Quick Corner Triangle directions on page 216. Sew a 1½" Fabric P square to each corner of a 3½" Fabric O square. Press. Make twenty.

O = 3½ x 3½
P = 1½ x 1½
Make 20

2. Sew 1½" Fabric P and 1½" Fabric Q squares together in pairs, referring to Quick Corner Triangle directions on page 216. Press. Make twenty.

P = 1½ x 1½
Q = 1½ x 1½
Make 20

3. Sew 1½" Fabric P square, 1½" Fabric R square, and one unit from step 2 to make a row. Press. Make twenty rows.

1½   1½   1½

Make 20

4. Sew units from step 1 to rows from step 3 as shown. Press. Block will measure 3½" x 4½".

5. Lay out four 4½" x 1½" Fabric P sashing pieces, four apple blocks, and one 4½" x 6½" Fabric P piece to make a horizontal row as shown. Sew blocks and strips together. Press. Make two rows.

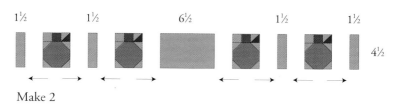

Make 2

6. Lay out six apple blocks, four 1½" x 3½" Fabric P sashing pieces, and one 4½" x 3½" Fabric P piece to make a vertical row as shown. Sew blocks and strips together. Press. Make two rows.

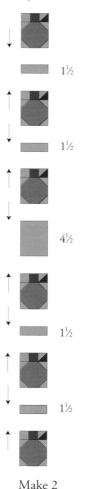

Make 2

7. Referring to layout on page 174 and color photo, sew units from step 5 to top and bottom of quilt. Press toward quilt center. Sew units from step 6 to sides. Press.

BORDERS

		Number of Strips	Dimensions
	MIDDLE BORDER	4	1½" x 42
	OUTSIDE BORDER	4	3½" x 42"
	BINDING	4	2¾" x 42"

1. Measure quilt through center from side to side. Trim two 1½" x 42" Fabric D middle border strips to this measurement. Sew to top and bottom. Press seams toward middle border.

2. Measure quilt through center from top to bottom, including border. Trim remaining 1½" x 42" Fabric D middle border strips to this measurement. Sew to sides. Press.

3. Repeat steps 1 and 2 to fit, trim, and sew 3½" x 42" outside border strips to top, bottom, and sides of quilt. Press seams toward outside border.

LAYERING AND FINISHING

1. Arrange and baste backing, batting, and top together, referring to Layering the Quilt directions on page 217.

2. Machine or hand quilt as desired.

3. Using the four 2¾" x 42" binding strips, refer to Binding the Quilt directions on page 217 to finish.

Apple Harvest

Apple Harvest
Finished Size: 20" x 23"
Photo: page 182

Whether you prefer *them red or green, sweet or tart, you'll find the apples in this yummy wallhanging hard to resist!*

Hang it in *your entry hall, country kitchen, or breakfast room to bring a touch of autumn's bounty indoors to enjoy. Read all instructions before beginning and use ¼" seams throughout.*

FABRIC REQUIREMENTS

Fabric A (Apples) - ⅛ yard or assorted scraps*
Fabric B (Background) - ⅛ yard
Fabric C (Stems) - Scraps
Fabric D (Leaves) - Scraps
Sashing - ⅙ yard
Corner Squares - ⅛ yard
Accent Border - ⅛ yard
Outside Border - ¼ yard

Binding - ⅜ yard
Backing - ¾ yard
Lightweight Batting - 24" x 27"
* We used one green and eight red fabrics.

CUTTING THE STRIPS AND PIECES

Read first paragraph of Cutting the Strips and Pieces on page 5.

		FIRST CUT		SECOND CUT	
		Number of Strips or Pieces	Dimensions	Number of Pieces	Dimensions
	FABRIC A	9	3½" squares		
	FABRIC B	2	1½" × 42"	54	1½" squares
	FABRIC C	9	1½" squares		
	FABRIC D	9	1½" squares		
	SASHING	3	1½" × 42"	12	1½" × 3½"
				12	1½" × 4½"
	CORNER SQUARES	1	1½" × 42"	16	1½" squares
	ACCENT BORDER	2	1" × 42"	2	1" × 13½"
				2	1" × 17½"
	OUTSIDE BORDER	2	3" × 42"	2	3" × 14½"
				2	3" × 22½"
	BINDING	3	2¾" × 42"		

MAKING THE APPLE BLOCKS

You will be making 9 apple blocks. Whenever possible, use the Asembly Line Method on page 5. Press in direction of arrows.

1. Refer to Quick Corner Triangle directions on page 216. Sew a 1½" Fabric B square to each corner of a 3½" Fabric A square. Press. Make nine.

A = 3½ × 3½
B = 1½ × 1½
Make 9

2. Sew 1½" Fabric B and 1½" Fabric D squares together in pairs, referring to Quick Corner Triangle directions on page 216. Press. Make nine.

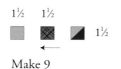

B = 1½ × 1½
D = 1½ × 1½
Make 9

3. Sew a remaining 1½" Fabric B square, a 1½" Fabric C square, and one unit from step 2 to make a row. Press. Make nine rows.

1½   1½

        1½

Make 9

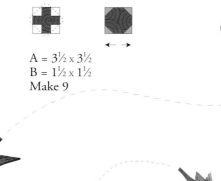

4. Sew a unit from step 1 to a row from step 3 as shown. Press. Make nine.

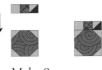

Make 9

ASSEMBLY

1. Lay out four 1½" x 4½" sashing strips and three apple blocks, alternating them to make a horizontal row as shown. Sew blocks and strips together. Press toward sashing. Make three rows, placing the green apple block in the center of one row.

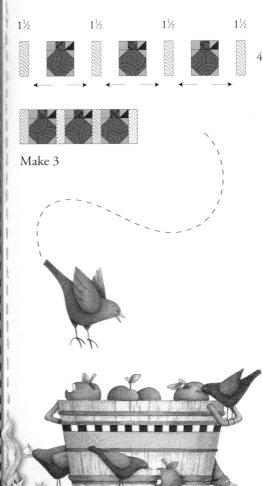

Make 3

2. Alternate four 1½" corner squares and three 1½" x 3½" sashing pieces to make a horizontal row as shown. Sew squares and strips together. Press toward sashing. Make four rows.

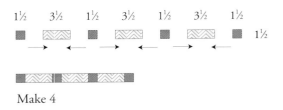

Make 4

3. Referring to layout on page 180 and color photo below, arrange rows from steps 1 and 2 as shown. Join rows and press.

BORDERS

Sew short accent borders to top and bottom of quilt. Press seams toward accent border. Sew long accent border strips to sides. Press. Repeat to add outside border strips to top, bottom, and sides. Press.

LAYERING AND FINISHING

1. Arrange and baste backing, batting, and top together, referring to Layering the Quilt directions on page 217.

2. Machine or hand quilt as desired.

3. Cut one 2¾" x 42" binding strip in half. Using shorter strips for top and bottom and longer strips for sides, refer to Binding the Quilt directions on page 217 to finish.

Class Act Wallhanging

Use photo transfer and a few quick construction changes to transform the "Apple Harvest" wall quilt into a wallhanging to give to a special teacher or administrator. You could use a snapshot of a class group, an old school house, or a delightful piece of artwork drawn by a child. Finished size will be 20" x 30".

CUTTING THE STRIPS AND PIECES

Fabric A - Six 3½" squares
Fabric B - Thirty-six 1½" squares
Fabric C - Six 1½" squares
Fabric D - Six 1½" squares
Fabric E (first photo border)
   Two 1" x 10½" pieces
   Two 1" x 9½" pieces
Fabric F (second photo border)
   Four 1½" x 11½" pieces
Sashing - Twelve 1½" x 3½" pieces
   Eight 1½" x 4½" pieces
Corner Squares - Sixteen 1½" squares

Accent Border - Two 1" x 13½" strips
   Two 1" x 24½" strips
Outside Border - Two 3" x 14½" strips
   Two 3" x 29½" strips
Photo transfer fabric - 12" x 14" piece
Binding - Three 2¾" x 42" strips
8" x 10" photo* or drawing

*Obtain photographer's permission if using professional photos

ASSEMBLY AND FINISHING

1. Photocopy a color or black and white image on image transfer paper following manufacturer's directions. Center and press on a 12" x 14" piece of fabric. A copy shop or scrapbook store may be able to make a better quality transfer for you. After transferring the image to fabric, trim the fabric to 10½" x 8½".

2. Sew the fabric photo between two 1" x 10½" Fabric E pieces. Press toward Fabric E. Sew two 1" x 9½" pieces to sides of fabric photo.

3. Repeat step 2 adding Fabric F pieces to top, bottom, and sides.

4. Follow instructions on page 181 and 182 to make six apple blocks. Follow instructions on page 182 to add sashing to apple blocks.

5. Sew unit from step 3 between apple block rows.

6. Continue following instructions on page 183 for Borders and Layering and Finishing using the sizes indicated for "Class Act" accent and outside borders.

Falling Leaves Table Runner & Placemats

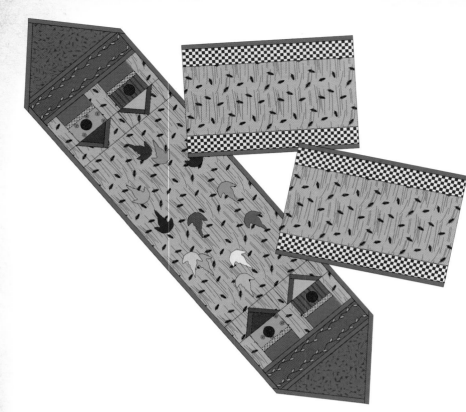

A sprinkling of *leaves in rich, earthy colors dance merrily across our charming table runner, signaling that autumn is near. Scrappy birdhouses and a whimsical print form the picture perfect frame.*

Why not whip *up a batch of our oh-so-easy autumn placemats to match? Read all instructions before beginning and use ¼"-wide seams throughout.*

Falling Leaves Table Runner & Placemats
Finished Table Runner Size: 14" x 59"
Finished Placemat Size: 19" x 13"
Photo: page 187

FABRIC REQUIREMENTS

Table Runner:
Birdhouses - Assorted scraps in a
   variety of colors
Fabric A (Background) - ⅝ yard
Fabric B (Trim) - ⅛ yard
Fabric C (Border) - ⅛ yard
Fabric D (Points) - ⅓ yard

Leaf Appliqués - Assorted scraps in a
   variety of colors
Binding - ⅜ yard *
Backing - ⅞ yard
Lightweight Batting - 18" x 62" piece

* May substitute 4 yards of doublefold
   bias tape.

CUTTING THE STRIPS AND PIECES

Read first paragraph of Cutting the Strips and Pieces on page 5.

	FIRST CUT		SECOND CUT	
	Number of Strips or Pieces	Dimensions	Number of Pieces	Dimensions
BIRDHOUSES	4	5½" x 3" (upper birdhouse)		
	4	4½" x 2" (birdhouse base)		
	4	4½" x 1" (birdhouse trim)		
	4	4½" x 2½" (middle birdhouse)		
	8	1" x 4½" (roof)		
	4	1½" squares (birdhouse holes)		
FABRIC A*	1	13½" x 24½"		
	8	3" squares		
	6	3" x 1½"		
	4	4½" x 2"		
	2	4½" x 2½"		
FABRIC B	2	1" x 42"	4	1" x 13½"
FABRIC C	1	3" x 42" (we used a "fussy cut" border)	2	3" x 13½"
FABRIC D	2	7½" x 14"		
BINDING	4	2¾" x 42"		

*We used directional fabric. Longer measurements are lengthwise.

MAKING THE BIRDHOUSE PANELS

You will be making two birdhouse panels to frame the appliquéd centerpiece of this project. Each panel includes two birdhouses made from a variety of scrap fabrics. Whenever possible, use the Assembly Line Method page on 5. Press in direction of arrows.

1. Refer to Quick Corner Triangle directions on page 216. Sew two 3" Fabric A squares to each 5½" x 3" upper birdhouse piece as shown. Press. Make four.

A = 3 x 3
Upper Birdhouse = 5½ x 3
Make 4

2. Sew three 3" x 1½" Fabric A pieces and two units from step 1 in order shown to make a horizontal row. Press. Make two.

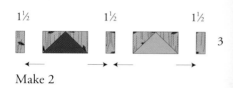

1½ 1½ 1½ 3

Make 2

3. Sew one 4½" x 1" birdhouse trim piece between one 4½" x 2" birdhouse base piece and one 4½" x 2½" middle birdhouse piece as shown. Press. Make four.

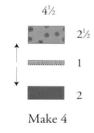

4½
2½
1
2

Make 4

4. Refer to layout on page 184 and color photo on page 187. Arrange and sew two 2" x 4½" Fabric A pieces, two units from step 3, and one 4½" x 2½" Fabric A piece in order shown to make a horizontal row. Press. Make two.

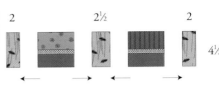

Make 2

5. Refer to layout and color photo. Sew rows from step 2 and step 4 together in pairs. Press. Make two panels. Panel will measure 13½" x 7".

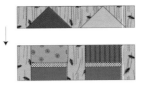

Make 2

6. Sew one 13½" x 3" Fabric C strip between two 13½" x 1" Fabric B strips. Press. Make two.

13½

1

3

1

Make 2

7. Sew units from step 6 to bottom edge of each panel from step 5. Press.

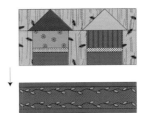

ASSEMBLY

1. Refer to layout on page 184 and color photo. Sew one birdhouse panel to each end of 13½"x 24½" Fabric A piece, taking care to position panels as shown. Press seams away from birdhouse panels.

2. Prepare points from Fabric D pieces. Fold each Fabric D piece in half along 14" side and press to mark center as shown. Align 45-degree mark on your ruler with center fold on each Fabric D piece. Trim away fabric triangle. Repeat on other side to create point.

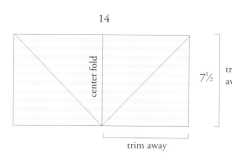

3. Refer to layout and color photo. Sew one Fabric D triangle to each end of unit from step 1. Press seams away from points.

APPLIQUÉ

1. Refer to Quick-fuse Appliqué directions on page 217. Trace appliqué designs from page 189. Fuse four birdhouse holes and twelve leaves.

2. Finish edges using a machine blanket, satin, or small zigzag stitch or if preferred, hand appliqué referring to directions on page 216. Appliqué two 1" x 4½" roof strips on each birdhouse. Follow seam lines and square ends as shown.

LAYERING AND FINISHING

1. Cut backing fabric lengthwise into two equal pieces. Sew pieces together to make one 20" x 62" (approximate) backing piece. Arrange and baste backing, batting, and top together, referring to Layering the Quilt directions on page 217.

2. Hand or machine quilt as desired. Trim batting ¼" from raw edge of table runner.

3. Sew 2¾" x 42" binding strips together end to end to make one continuous 2¾" wide strip. From this strip, cut two 2¾" x 48" (approximate) binding strips. Sew these strips to long sides, extending strips at both ends as shown. Press binding away from table runner. Following angle of short sides, trim excess length of binding.

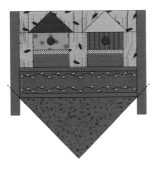

4. Cut four 2¾" x 12" binding strips from remaining 2¾"-wide strip. Sew one short binding strip to one side of each point. Press binding away from table runner. Trim excess length ¼" away from folded edge of side binding strip and even with raw edge on other end.

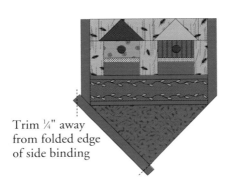

Trim ¼" away from folded edge of side binding

5. Sew remaining short binding strips to remaining sides. Press and trim ¼" away from folded edge of side binding strip and even with folded edge of binding strip on pointed end.

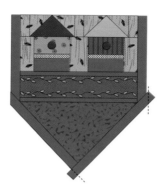

6. Press binding to back. Fold long sides first, then short sides with raw edge, then finally short sides with folded edge around to back. Press, pin in position, and hand stitch binding in place.

Birdhouse hole for
Falling Leaves Table Runner

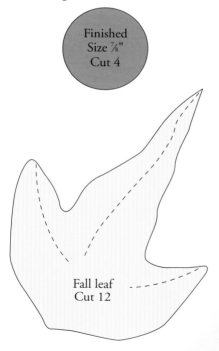

Finished
Size ⅞"
Cut 4

Fall leaf
Cut 12

Falling Leaves Placemats

These sweet 'n simple placemats partner perfectly with our table runner (see page 187). If you'd like, use the leaf pattern to trace, cut, and appliqué three or more leaves to each placemat center. Fabric requirements and cutting instructions are for a single placemat; make as many as you need for your harvest table. Read all instructions before beginning and use ¼"-wide seams throughout. Finished size will be 19" x 13".

FABRIC REQUIREMENTS

One Placemat:
Placemat Center - 19½" x 8½" piece
Border - Two 19½" x 2½" strips*
Binding - Two 2¾" x 20" strips
Backing - 24" x 17" piece

Lightweight Batting - 24" x 17" piece
* We chose a fussy cut for the border. If you choose to do the same, you may need to adjust the size of the placemat center.

ASSEMBLY AND FINISHING

1. Sew 19½" x 8½" placemat center piece between two 19½" x 2½" border strips. Press toward borders.

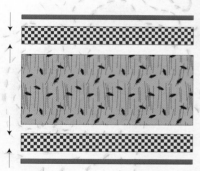

2. Position top and backing right sides together. Center both pieces on top of batting and pin all three layers together. Using ¼" seams, sew both 12½" edges.

3. Trim stitched seams, turn placemats right side out, trim batting and backing ¼" from raw edge of placemat top.

4. Machine or hand quilt as desired.

5. Sew 2¾" x 20" binding strips to long edges, leaving ½" seam allowance extending beyond each end. Fold binding in half turning to back and press, tucking in raw edges to finish ends. Pin and hand stitch binding in place.

Winter

Outside the snow may be falling and the wintry wind blowing ... but inside it's cozy and warm. Our heartier feathered friends find shelter in their snow-capped homes. Bright cardinals flit across the frosty ground on their winter rounds while cheery chickadees add sweet songs to the snowy stillness.

You, too, can nestle snugly into wintertime. Just wrap yourself in a cozy quilt and enjoy working on these wonderful winter projects for your home. Outside the window—let it snow, let it snow!

Birdhouse Border Christmas Quilt

Birdhouse Border Christmas Quilt

Finished Quilt Size: 61" square

Photo: page 194

Holiday time

means a house brimming with loved ones, and an extra quilt is always welcome! No matter who is home for the holidays at your house, we're sure this clever quilt will be admired ... and happily used for years to come.

Read all instructions

before beginning and use ¼" seams throughout.

FABRIC REQUIREMENTS

Fabric A (Irish Chain) - ⅓ yard
Fabric B (Irish Chain) - ⅓ yard
Fabric C (Irish Chain Centers)
  ⅛ yard
Fabric D (Irish Chain) - ⅓ yard
Fabric E (Irish Chain) - ⅝ yard
Fabric F (Irish Chain and Star)
  1 yard
Fabric G (Star Points) - ½ yard
Fabric H (Star Corners) - ¼ yard
Fabric I (Star Centers) - ½ yard
Fabric J (Corner Stars) - ⅛ yard
Fabric K (Corner Star Points) - ⅛ yard
Fabric L (Corner Star Centers)
  Scraps
Accent Border - ⅓ yard
Outside Border - ⅞ yard*

Binding - ⅔ yard
Backing - 4⅛ yard
Lightweight Batting - 69" x 69" piece

*If you select a border print as we did, you will need to increase the yardage, depending on the number of design repeats in the fabric.

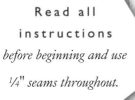

CUTTING THE STRIPS AND PIECES

Read first paragraph of Cutting the Strips and Pieces on page 5.

		FIRST CUT		SECOND CUT	
		Number of Strips or Pieces	Dimensions	Number of Pieces	Dimensions
■	FABRIC A AND FABRIC B	4	2½" x 42" each color		
▦	FABRIC C	1	2½" x 42"		
☐	FABRIC D	4	2½" x 42"		
☐	FABRIC E	8	2½" x 42"		
▨	FABRIC F	4 8	2½" x 42" 2½" x 42"	48	2½" x 6½"
■	FABRIC G	6	2½" x 42"	96	2½" squares
■	FABRIC H	3	2½" x 42"	48	2½" squares
☐	FABRIC I	2	6½" x 42"	12	6½" squares
■	FABRIC J	2	1½" x 42"	16 16	1½" x 2½" 1½" squares
☐	FABRIC K	2	1½" x 42"	32	1½" squares
▨	FABRIC L	4	2½" squares		
■	ACCENT BORDER	6	1½" x 42"		
◀	OUTSIDE BORDER	6	4½" x 42"		
■	BINDING	8	2¾" x 42"		

MAKING THE BLOCKS

You will be making 13 Irish Chain blocks, 12 star blocks, and four small corner star blocks. Whenever possible, use the Assembly Line Method page 5. Press in direction of arrows.

Irish Chain Blocks

1. Sew 2½" x 42" strips together in the following order to make two identical strip sets: Fabric A, Fabric E, Fabric F, Fabric E, and Fabric A.* Press. Cut twenty-six 2½"segments.

*Sew each strip in opposite directions to prevent stretching.

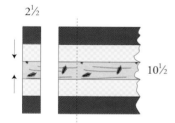

Make 2 strip sets
Cut 26

2. Repeat to sew 2½" x 42" strips together in the following order to make two identical strips sets: Fabric E, Fabric B, Fabric D, Fabric B, and Fabric E.* Press. Cut twenty-six 2½" segments.

*Sew each strip in opposite directions to prevent stretching.

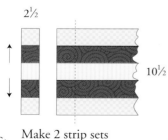

Make 2 strip sets
Cut 26

3. Sew 2½" x 42" strips together in the following order to make one strip set: Fabric F, Fabric D, Fabric C, Fabric D, and Fabric F.* Press. Cut thirteen 2½" segments.

   *Sew each strip in opposite directions to prevent stretching.

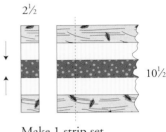

Make 1 strip set
Cut 13

4. Arrange two units from step 1, two units from step 2, and one unit from step 3 as shown. Sew rows together, carefully matching seams. Press. Make thirteen blocks.

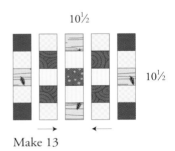

Make 13

Star Blocks

1. Refer to Quick Corner Triangle directions on page 216. Sew two 2½" Fabric G squares to each 2½" x 6½" Fabric F strip as shown. Press. Make forty-eight.

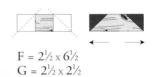

F = 2½ x 6½
G = 2½ x 2½
Make 48

2. Sew each 6½" Fabric I square between two units from step 1 as shown. Press. Make twelve.

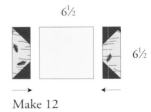

Make 12

3. Sew each remaining unit from step 1 between two 2½" Fabric H squares as shown. Press. Make twenty-four.

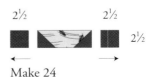

Make 24

4. Sew each unit from step 2 between two units from step 3. Press. Block measures 10½". Make twelve.

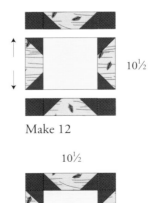

Make 12

ASSEMBLY

1. Refer to layout on page 192 and color photo. Alternate three Irish Chain blocks and two star blocks to make a horizontal row. Sew blocks together. Press seams toward Irish Chain blocks. Make three rows.

2. Refer to layout on page 192 and color photo. Alternate three star blocks and two Irish Chain blocks to make a horizontal row. Sew blocks together. Press seams toward Irish Chain Blocks. Make two rows.

3. Referring to the layout on page 192 and the color photo, lay out the rows from steps 1 and 2 as shown. Join the rows and press.

Corner Star Blocks

1. Refer to Quick Corner Triangle directions on page 216. Sew two 1½" Fabric K squares to each 1½" x 2½" Fabric J strip as shown. Press. Make sixteen.

J = 1½ x 2½
K = 1½ x 1½
Make 16

2. Sew each 2½" Fabric L square between two units from step 1 as shown. Press. Make four.

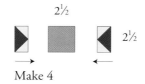

2½

2½

Make 4

3. Sew each remaining unit from step 1 between two 1½" Fabric J squares as shown. Press. Make eight.

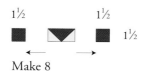

1½   1½

1½

Make 8

4. Sew each unit from step 2 between two units from step 3. Press. Make four.

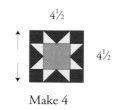

4½

4½

Make 4

BORDERS

1. Sew 1½" x 42" accent border strips end to end to make one continuous 1½"-wide strip. Measure quilt through center from side to side. Cut two 1½"-wide accent border strips to that measurement. Sew to top and bottom. Press seams toward border strips.

2. Measure quilt through center from top to bottom, including borders just added. Cut two 1½"-wide accent border strips to that measurement. Sew to sides. Press.

3. Sew 4½" x 42" outside border strips end to end to make one continuous 4½"-wide strip. Measure quilt through center from side to side, and from top to bottom. (This measurement should be the same.) Cut four 4½"-wide outside border strips to that measurement.

4. Sew two 4½"-wide outside border strips to top and bottom edges of quilt. Press.

5. Sew a corner star block to the ends of two remaining 4½"-wide outside border strips. Press seams toward border strips.

6. Sew borders from step 5 to sides of quilt. Press.

LAYERING AND FINISHING

1. Cut backing fabric crosswise into two equal pieces. Sew pieces together to make one 75" x 75" (approximate) backing piece. Arrange and baste backing, batting, and top together, referring to Layering the Quilt directions on page 217.

2. Machine or hand quilt as desired. On pages 196-197 we have provided quilting templates of bird houses which we used on the 6½" Fabric I squares.

3. Sew 2¾" x 42" binding strips in pairs. Refer to Binding the Quilt directions on page 217 and use the pieced binding strips to finish.

Quilting template
placement for blocks

QUILTING TEMPLATES

Use on the 6½" Fabric I squares, if desired, for the Birdhouse Border Christmas Quilt.

To transfer the quilting templates to your quilt top:

1. Trace the template designs onto 6-inch squares of lightweight, tear-away stabilizer.

2. Place the traced template over the center block square and attach by using a temporary fabric adhesive or pins.

3. Machine stitch on the traced lines, starting in the center and continuing toward the edges.

4. Carefully tear away the stabilizer. (Waxed butcher paper may be used in place of the stabilizer. Trace the design onto the paper side of the butcher paper and press the paper to the block with a warm iron. Continue as above.)

Crimson Cardinals Table Quilt

Crimson Cardinals Table Quilt
Finished Table Quilt Size: 41" square
Photo: page 201

Just as nature's *cardinals accent the winter landscape, our four bright red cardinals add a splash of vibrant color to this striking table topper.*

Instructions are for *hand appliqué techniques, but you can substitute quick-fuse methods if you prefer. Read all instructions before beginning and use ¼" seams throughout.*

FABRIC REQUIREMENTS

Fabric A (Center Block) - ½ yard
Fabric B (Dark Red Center and
   Sawtooth Border Triangles) - ⅞ yard
Fabric C (Tan Triangles) - ⅓ yard
Fabric D (Medium Red Triangles)
   ½ yard
Fabric E (Medium Green Triangles)
   ⅝ yard
Fabric F (Dark Green Corner
   Triangles) - ⅓ yard
Fabric G (Green Sawtooth Border
   Triangles) - ⅔ yard

Accent Border - ⅛ yard
Appliqués - Assorted red scraps
   for cardinal bodies and wings
Binding - ½ yard
Backing - 1¼ yards *
Lightweight Batting - 44" x 44" piece
Black Embroidery Floss

* Fabric must measure 45" wide.

CUTTING THE STRIPS AND PIECES

Read first paragraph of Cutting the Strips and Pieces on page 5.

	FIRST CUT		SECOND CUT	
	Number of Strips or Pieces	Dimensions	Number of Pieces	Dimensions
FABRIC A	1	15½" square		
FABRIC B	6	4½" × 42"	44	4½" squares
FABRIC C	2	4½" × 42"	4 8	4½" × 8½" 4½" squares
FABRIC D	3	4½" × 42"	12	4½" × 8½"
FABRIC E	2 1	4½" × 42" 8½" × 42"	16 4	4½" squares 8½" squares
FABRIC F	1	8½" × 42"	4	8½" squares
FABRIC G	5	4½" × 42"	4 28	4½" × 8½" 4½" squares
ACCENT BORDER	2	1" × 42"	2 2	1" × 15½" 1" × 16½"
BINDING	5	2¾" × 42"		

MAKING THE CENTER PANEL

Whenever possible use the Assembly Line Method on page 5. Press in direction of arrows.

1. Sew 1" x 15½" accent border strips to opposite sides of 15½" Fabric A center block. Press seams toward accent border. Sew 1" x 16½" accent border strips to two remaining sides of block. Press.

2. Refer to Quick Corner Triangle directions on page 216. Sew two 4½" Fabric B squares to each 4½" x 8½" Fabric C piece as shown. Press. Make four.

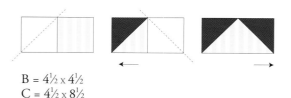

B = 4½ x 4½
C = 4½ x 8½
Make 4

3. Sew two 4½" Fabric E squares to one 4½" x 8½" Fabric D piece as shown. Press. Make four.

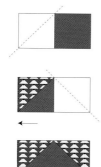

D = 4½ x 8½
E = 4½ x 4½
Make 4

4. Sew units from step 2 and step 3 together in pairs as shown. Press. Make four.

Make 4

5. Sew one 4½" Fabric C square and one 4½" Fabric E square to each remaining 4½" x 8½" Fabric D pieces as shown. Press. Make four of each variation.

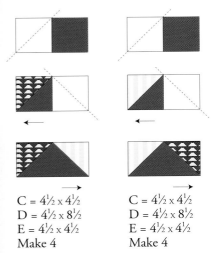

C = 4½ x 4½
D = 4½ x 8½
E = 4½ x 4½
Make 4

C = 4½ x 4½
D = 4½ x 8½
E = 4½ x 4½
Make 4

6. Sew each unit from step 4 between one of each unit from step 5 as shown. Press. Make four.

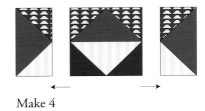

Make 4

7. Sew 8½" Fabric E and 8½" Fabric F squares together in pairs, referring to Quick Corner Triangle directions on page 216. Press. Make four.

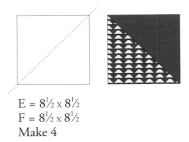

E = 8½ x 8½
F = 8½ x 8½
Make 4

8. Sew one unit from step 6 between two units from step 7 as shown. Press. Make two. Strip measures 32½" x 8½".

Make 2

9. Sew remaining units from step 6 to opposite sides of bordered center block. Press.

10. Sew units from step 8 to remaining sides. Press to outside.

Cardinal Appliqués

1. Trace appliqué designs from page 202. Make templates and use red scraps to trace four each of pieces 1 (under wing), 2 (body), 3 (top wing), and use gold or yellow fabric to trace four of piece 4 (beak). Cut out appliqués, adding ¼" seam allowance around each piece.

2. Referring to layout on page 198 and color photo, position appliqués in four corners of center block. Refer to Hand Appliqué directions on page 216 to stitch appliqués in place.

3. Referring to pattern on page 202 for placement, use two strands of black embroidery floss to make French knot eye for each cardinal. Add additional embroidered detail as desired. Refer to Embroidery Stitch Guide on page 216.

Sawtooth Border

1. Refer to Quick Corner Triangle directions on page 216. Sew two 4½" Fabric B squares to each 4½" x 8½" Fabric G piece as shown. Press. Make four.

B = 4½ x 4½
C = 4½ x 8½
Make 4

2. Sew remaining 4½" Fabric B and 4½" Fabric G squares together in pairs, referring to Quick Corner Triangle directions on page 216. Press. Make twenty-eight.

B = 4½ x 4½
G = 4½ x 4½
Make 28

3. Sew one unit from step 1 and six units from step 2 as shown. Press. Make four.

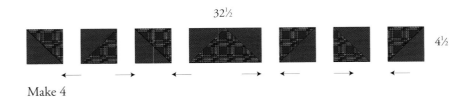

32½

4½

Make 4

4. Referring to layout on page 198 and color photo on page 201, sew two units from step 3 to opposite sides of quilt. Press seams away from center panel.

5. Sew each remaining unit from step 3 between remaining units from step 2. Press.

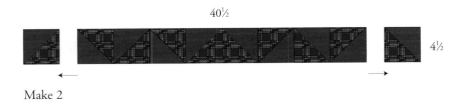

40½

4½

Make 2

6. Sew units from step 5 to remaining sides of quilt. Press.

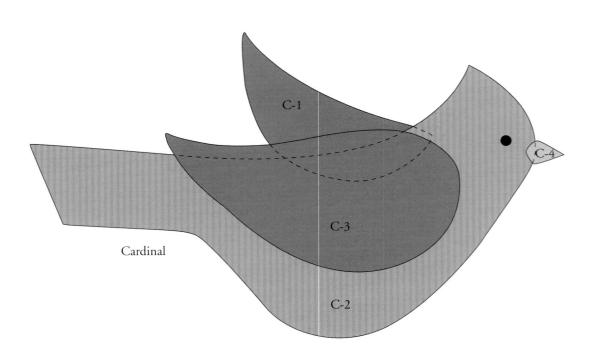

C-1

C-4

C-3

Cardinal

C-2

LAYERING AND FINISHING

1. Arrange and baste backing, batting, and top together, referring to Layering the Quilt directions on page 217.

2. Machine or hand quilt as desired.

3. Using the five 2¾" x 42" binding strips, refer to Binding the Quilt directions on page 217 to finish.

Birdfeeder

Here's a great wintertime treat for our feathered friends! Upside down feeders such as the nuthatch particularly enjoy it.

MATERIALS
Pinecones
Bird Seed
Bacon grease or other fat
Peanut Butter

1. Stir equal portions of peanut butter, bacon grease or other discarded fat, and bird seed.

2. Tie a sturdy string to fir cones or pinecones and roll in mixture.

3. Hang from a tree limb.

Winter Birds Mantel Cover

Winter Birds Mantel Cover
Finished Panel Size: 8" x 18"
Photo: page 206

A fragrant, crackling fire *becomes even more inviting when your mantel is dressed in our charming four-panel mantel topper. We've hand appliquéd the birds, or you can quick-fuse them as we have the snowflakes and flowers.*

It's up to you! *We've also included tips for easily hanging this wonderful wintertime creation. Read all instructions before beginning and use ¼" seams throughout.*

FABRIC REQUIREMENTS

Background - 1 yard *
Appliqués - Assorted scraps for birds, snowflakes, and poinsettias
Binding - ½ yard
Embroidery Floss

Lightweight Batting - Four 10" x 20" pieces (optional)

* May substitute ¼ yard each of four different green fabrics.

CUTTING THE STRIPS AND PIECES

Read first paragraph of Cutting the Strips and Pieces on page 5.

		FIRST CUT		SECOND CUT	
		Number of Strips or Pieces	Dimensions	Number of Pieces	Dimensions
	BACK-GROUND	4	8" x 36"		
	BINDING	5	2¾" x 42"	8	2¾" x 15"
				8	2¾" x 10"

PREPARING BACKGROUND PANELS

1. Fold each 8" x 36" background panel in half lengthwise and press to mark center as shown. Align 45-degree mark on your ruler with center fold on background fabric. Trim away fabric triangle on one short end of background fabric. Repeat on other end to create points.

4

center fold

36

2. Repeat step 1 on other 8" ends of each background panel.

APPLIQUE AND EMBROIDERY

1. Refer to Quick-Fuse Appliqué directions on page 216. Trace appliqué designs for pieces 1-3 on page 207. Prepare two of piece 1 (snowflake), and four each of pieces 2 and 3 (poinsettia).

2. Refer to layout on page 204 and color photo on page 206. Center and fuse one snowflake appliqué 2½" from one point on two background panels.

3. Center, stack, and fuse two of each poinsettia appliqués 2½" from one point on each remaining background panel.

4. Trace appliqué designs for cardinal, wren, junco, and goldfinch from pages 202, 207, and 214. Make templates and use scraps to trace one of each pattern piece. Cut out appliqués, add ¼" seam allowance around each piece if using hand appliqué. If using Quick-fuse method reverse bird appliqué patterns.

5. Referring to pattern layout on page 204, and color photo on page 206, position one bird on each panel.

6. Machine stitch or refer to Hand Appliqué on page 216. Stitch appliqués in place. Begin with Piece 1 and work numerically as indicated on patterns.

7. Use two strands of yellow embroidery floss to make french knot centers for each poinsettia. Use two strands of black embroidery floss to make french knot eye for each bird. Add additional embroidered detail as desired. Refer to Embroidery Stitch Guide on page 216.

ASSEMBLY AND FINISHING

1. Fold background fabric in half wrong sides together, matching points as shown. Press the fold. Place a lightweight batting in center flush with fold. Hand or pin baste through all layers, and baste around cut edges.

fold

2. Hand or machine quilt as desired.

3. Trim batting to ¼" from raw edges of mantel covers.

4. Sew 2¾" x 15" binding strips to long sides of each panel. Extend strip ¼" past folded edge, and leave excess extending beyond bottom edge as shown. Press binding away from panel. Following angle of short sides, trim excess length of binding on bottom edge only.

5. Sew one 2¾" x 10" binding strip to one side of each point. Press binding away from panel. Trim excess length ¼" away from folded edge of side binding strip and even with raw edge on other end. Press to outside edges.

Trim ¼" away from folded edge of side binding

6. Sew remaining short binding strips to remaining side of each point. Press and trim ¼" away from folded edge of side binding strip and even with folded edge of binding strip on pointed end.

7. Press binding to outside. Fold long sides first, then short sides with raw edge, and finally short sides with folded edge around to back. Pin and hand stitch binding in place.

Make a display

To display your mantel covers, place four inches on the mantle and allow the rest to hang. You may set your decorations on top to hold the covers in place, secure with tape; or attach velcro flush with and 4" from the folded edge, fasten the velcro and insert a narrow rod or slat to secure.

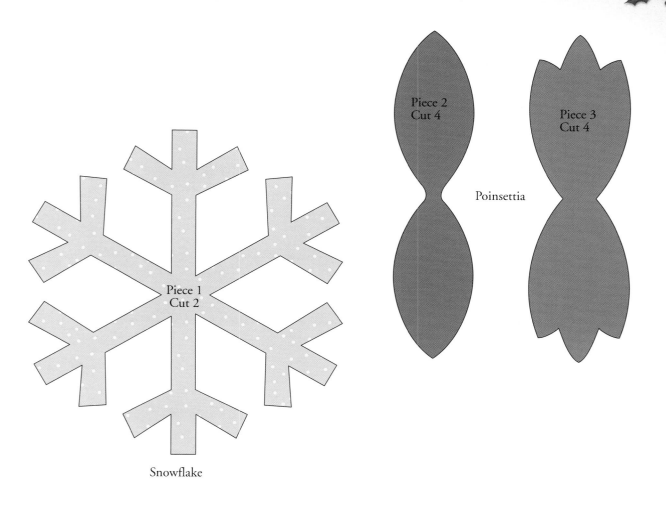

Piece 2
Cut 4

Piece 3
Cut 4

Poinsettia

Piece 1
Cut 2

Snowflake

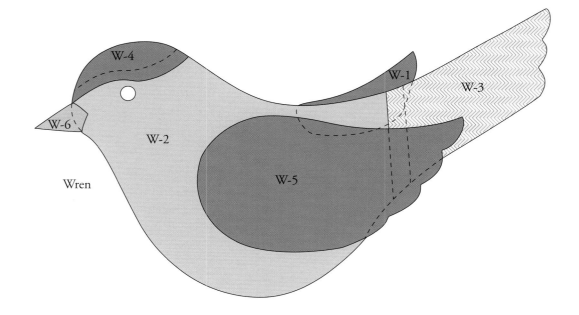

W-4

W-1

W-3

W-6

W-2

W-5

Wren

Birdhouse Banner

Birdhouse Banner
Finished Quilt Size: 21" x 23½"
Photos: pages 210 and 211

Here's a clever idea ... a bright and beautiful birdhouse banner with easy-to-change trims to welcome each season. There are three methods for creating the various seasonal adornments and three ways to attach them.

Choose the option

you like best! Read all instructions before beginning and use ¼" seams throughout.

FABRIC REQUIREMENTS

Fabric A (Roof and Chimney Top) ⅛ yard

Fabric B (Background) - ¼ yard

Fabric C (Branches) - Scraps

Fabric D (House) - ⅙ yard

Fabric E (Shutters) - Scraps

Fabric F (Door Trim) - Scraps

Fabric G (Door) - Scrap

Fabric H (House Trim) - Scraps

Fabric I (House Base and Chimney) ⅛ yard

Fabric J (Birdhouse Stand and Post) ⅛ yard

Birdhouse Hole Appliqué - Scrap

Birds and Other Seasonal Trims - Assorted Scraps

Accent Border - ⅛ yard

Outside Border - ¼ yard

Binding - ⅓ yard

Backing - ⅞ yard

Lightweight Batting - 23" x 26" piece

Embroidery Floss

Scraps of heavy-duty fusible web

Scraps of lightweight batting (optional) *

Assorted small buttons (optional) *

Small hooks *

* Whether you need these notions will be determined by the methods you choose to construct and attach the birds and other seasonal trims. See pages 212 and 213.

CUTTING THE STRIPS AND PIECES

Read first paragraph of Cutting the Strips and Pieces on page 5.

		FIRST CUT		SECOND CUT	
		Number of Strips or Pieces	Dimensions	Number of Pieces	Dimensions
■	FABRIC A	2	1" x 42"	1 1 1 1 1 1 1	8½" x 1" 9" x 1" 9½" x 1" 10" x 1" 10½" x 1" 11" x 1" 3" x 1"
▨	FABRIC B	1	1" x 42"	14 2 2 2 2	1" squares 1¾" x 1" 1½" x 1" 1¼" x 1" ¾" x 1"
		2 2 2 2 1	2¾" x 3½" 3" x 8½" 7¼" x 2" 7" x 2" 15½" x 2½"		
■	FABRIC C	1	1¼" x 20"	Bias cut recommended	
▦	FABRIC D	2 1 2 2	3¼" x 2¾" 2½" x 2¾" 3¾" x 4¼" 9½" x 1"		
■	FABRIC E	2	1¼" x 2¾"		
■	FABRIC F	1 2	2½" x ¾" ¾" x 4¼"		
▨	FABRIC G	1	2½" x 4"		
■	FABRIC H	2	1" x 7½"		
▦	FABRIC I	1 1	10½" x 1½" 2½" x 2"		
■	FABRIC J	1 1	2" square 15½" x 2"		
■	ACCENT BORDER	2	1" x 42"	2 2	1" x 15½" 1" x 19"
■	OUTSIDE BORDER	2	2½" x 42"	2 2	2½" x 16½" 2½" x 23"
	BACKING	1	24" x 27"		
■	BINDING	3	2¾" x 42"		

MAKING THE BIRDHOUSE BLOCK

You will be making one birdhouse block. Whenever possible, use the Assembly Line Method on page 216 for each step. Press in direction of arrows.

Helpful Hint

Since this block involves many similarly sized (but not identical) pieces, you may wish to label each piece with masking tape marked with its measurements.

1. Refer to Quick Corner Triangle directions on page 216. Sew two 1" Fabric B squares to 8½" x 1" Fabric A strip, and label pieced strip as shown. Press. Repeat to sew two 1" Fabric B squares to 9" x 1" Fabric A strip, 9½" x 1" Fabric A strip, 10" x 1" Fabric A strip, 10½"x 1" Fabric A strip, and 11" x 1" Fabric A strip. Label and press.

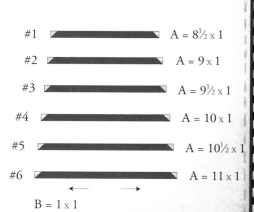

#1   A = 8½ x 1
#2   A = 9 x 1
#3   A = 9½ x 1
#4   A = 10 x 1
#5   A = 10½ x 1
#6   A = 11 x 1

B = 1 x 1

2. Using strips pieced in step 1, sew strip #1 between two 1¾" x 1" Fabric B pieces as shown. Press. Repeat to sew strip #2 between two 1½" x 1" Fabric B pieces, strip #3 between two 1¼" x 1" Fabric B pieces, strip #4 between two 1" Fabric B squares, and strip #5 between two ¾" x 1" Fabric B pieces. Press.

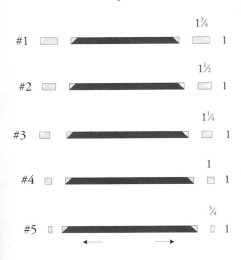

3. Arrange and sew roof strips 1-5 and #6 from step 1 in order shown to make a vertical row. Press. Unit will measure 11" x 3½".

4. Sew unit from step 3 between two 2¾" x 3½" Fabric B pieces as shown. Press.

5. Arrange and sew two 3¼" x 2¾" Fabric D pieces, two 1¼" x 2¾" Fabric E pieces, and one 2½" x 2¾" Fabric D piece in order shown to make a horizontal row. Press.

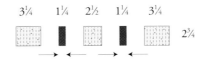

6. Sew 2½" x ¾" Fabric F piece to 2½" x 4" Fabric G piece as shown. Press.

7. Sew unit from step 6 between two ¾" x 4¼" Fabric F pieces. Press.

8. Sew unit from step 7 between two 3¾" x 4¼" Fabric D pieces. Press.

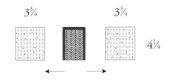

9. Arrange and sew one 9½" x 1" Fabric D strip, unit from step 5, remaining 9½" x 1" Fabric D strip, and unit from step 8 in order shown to make a vertical row. Press.

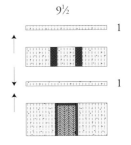

10. Sew unit from step 9 between two 1" x 7½" Fabric H strips. Press.

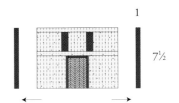

Summer Birdhouse Banner with Peaches and Finches

11. Sew 10½" x 1½" Fabric I strip to unit from step 10 as shown. Press.

10½

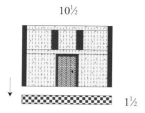

1½

12. Sew unit from step 11 between two 3" x 8½" Fabric B pieces. Press.

3

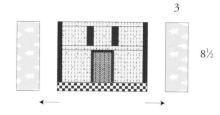

8½

13. Sew 2" Fabric J square between two 7¼" x 2" Fabric B pieces. Press.

7¼   2   7¼

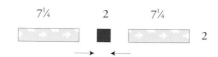   2

14. Sew 15½" x 2" Fabric J strip to unit from step 13 as shown. Press.

15½

   2

15. Sew 2½" x 2" Fabric I piece between two 7" x 2" Fabric B pieces. Press.

7   2½   7

   2

16. Arrange and sew 15½" x 2½" Fabric B strip, unit from step 15, unit from step 4, unit from step 12, and unit from step 14 in order shown to make a vertical row. Press.

15½

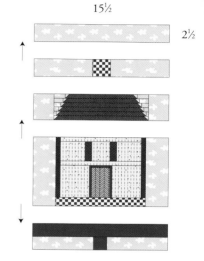   2½

Spring Birdhouse Banner with Dogwood and Bluebirds

Autumn Birdhouse Banner with Maples and Juncos

Winter Birdhouse Banner with Holly and Cardinals

17. Trace birdhouse hole appliqué design from page 215. Make template and use scrap to cut one birdhouse hole, adding ¼" seam allowance.

18. Refer to Hand Appliqué directions on page 216. Referring to layout on page 208 and color photo on page 211, appliqué 3" x 1" chimney top over chimney, and birdhouse hole between shutters on house front. Position and appliqué branches to block background, trimming 1¼" x 20" bias strip into segments as needed.

BORDERS

1. Sew 1" x 15½" accent border strips to top and bottom of block. Press toward border strips. Repeat to sew 1" x 19" accent border strips to sides. Press.

2. Sew 2½" x 16½" outside border strips to top and bottom. Press toward outside border strips. Repeat to sew 2½" x 23" outside border strips to sides. Press.

LAYERING AND FINISHING

1. Arrange and baste backing, batting, and top together referring to Layering the Quilt directions on page 217.

2. Hand or machine quilt as desired.

3. Sew 2¾" x 42" binding strips end to end to make one continuous 2¾"-wide binding strip. Refer to Binding the Quilt directions on page 217 to finish.

Tip

Details such as bird wings may be assembled (layered, traced, stitched, and cut) separately, then tacked to main piece.

SEASONAL TRIMS

We used three methods for making birds and other seasonal trims for the banner. You may use one method, or any combination, to create the various trims.

Method 1:

1. We used this method for the dogwood leaf, peach leaf, and fall leaf. Refer to patterns for birds and seasonal trims on pages 202, 214, and 215. Make templates and trace required number of pieces onto heavy-duty fusible web. Follow manufacturer's directions to iron fusible web to wrong side of appropriately colored scraps. Cut designs along traced lines.

2. Cut a 6" square (approximate) of fabric to match main fabric in bird or seasonal trim. Fuse pieces from step 1 to wrong side of appropriate 6" square, layering them in numerical order as indicated on pattern.

3. Cut out bird or seasonal trim along outside edge of finished shape.

4. Refer to pattern, and use three strands of embroidery floss to make birds' eyes, and/or add other details. Refer to Embroidery Stitch Guide on page 216.

Method 2:

1. We used this method for peaches and dogwood blossoms. Refer to patterns for birds and seasonal trims on pages 202, 214, and 215. Trace required number of complete bird or seasonal trim outlines onto dull side of freezer paper.

2. Cut two matching 6" squares (approximate) of main bird or seasonal trim fabric. Layer as for quilting (one 6" square right side down, batting, one 6" square right side up).

3. Use a warm iron to press freezer paper shiny side down on top side of appropriate fabric "sandwich." Stitch directly on traced line, using a small stitch.

4. Remove freezer paper. Trim close to stitching with straight edge or pinking shears.

5. Follow manufacturer's directions and use fusible web to trace and fuse beaks, breasts, wings, and tails to bird bodies, and details to seasonal trims.

6. Refer to pattern, and use three strands of embroidery floss to make birds' eyes, and/or add other details. Refer to Embroidery Stitch Guide on page 216.

Tips

Buttons may be substituted for dogwood centers and holly berries.

In some cases, fabrics may be stitched together before tracing and cutting; such as for goldfinch body and tail, etc.

Method 3:

1. We used this method for the birds and holly leaves. Refer to patterns for birds and seasonal trims on pages 202, 214, and 215. Trace one complete bird or seasonal trim outline onto template material.

2. Cut two matching 6" squares (approximate) of main bird or seasonal trim fabric. Place squares right sides together, and layer over 6" square of thin batting.

3. Place full outline template on wrong side of top fabric and trace. Stitch on traced lines, using a small stitch.

4. Trim close to stitching. Cut a small slit in top fabric only, and turn right side out.

5. Follow manufacturer's directions and use fusible web to trace and fuse beaks, breasts, wings, and tails to bird bodies, and details to seasonal trims.

6. Refer to pattern, and use three strands of embroidery floss to make birds' eyes, and/or add other details. Refer to Embroidery Stitch Guide on page 216.

ATTACHING TRIMS

You may use one of three methods to attach birds and trims to banner. Refer to layout on page 208, and color photos on page 210 and 211 for placement guidance as needed.

Method 1:

Sew buttons to banner as indicated. Make buttonholes in trims to attach.

Method 2:

Sew buttons to banner as indicated. Sew thread loop to back of each trim. Hook loops over buttons to attach.

Method 3:

Sew 3/8" thread loops to branches and background as desired. Attach hook to back of each trim. Hook trim to thread loop on banner.

● Indicates button placement

◆ Indicates loop placement

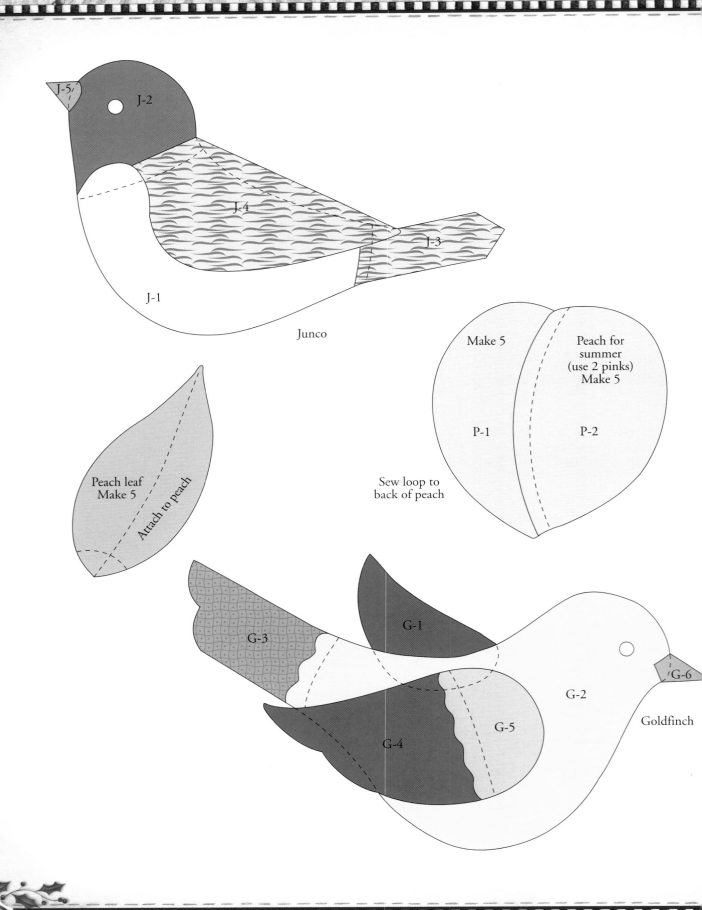

J-5

J-2

J-4

J-3

J-1

Junco

Peach leaf
Make 5

Attach to peach

Make 5

Peach for
summer
(use 2 pinks)
Make 5

P-1

P-2

Sew loop to
back of peach

G-3

G-1

G-6

G-2

G-5

G-4

Goldfinch

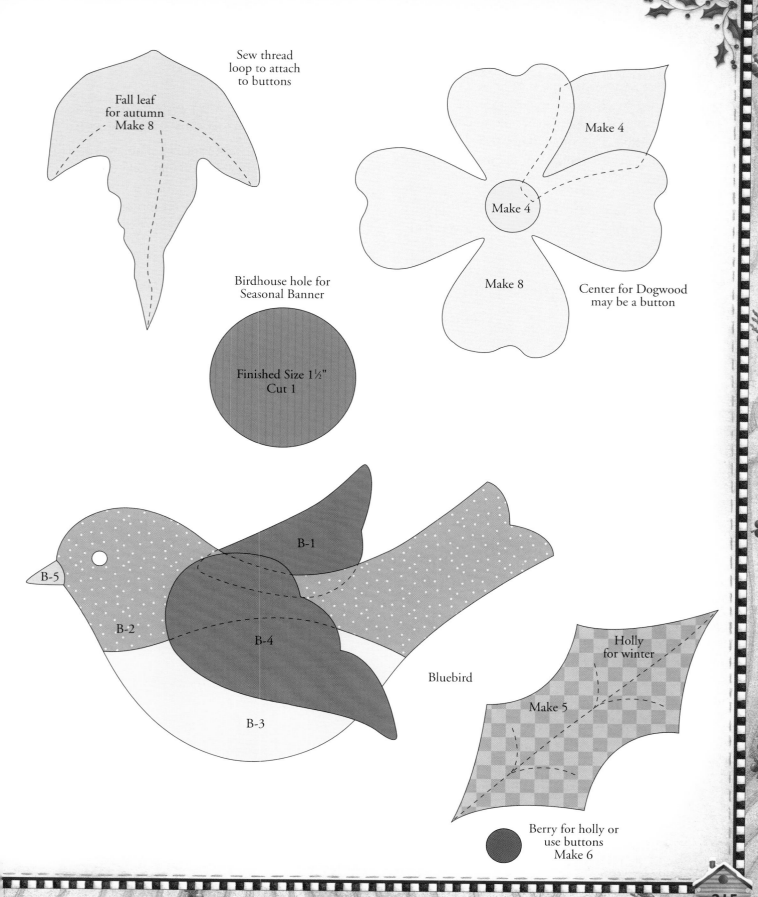

Sew thread
loop to attach
to buttons

Fall leaf
for autumn
Make 8

Make 4

Make 4

Birdhouse hole for
Seasonal Banner

Make 8

Center for Dogwood
may be a button

Finished Size 1½"
Cut 1

B-1

B-5

Holly
for winter

B-2

B-4

Make 5

Bluebird

B-3

Berry for holly or
use buttons
Make 6

HAND APPLIQUÉ

Hand appliqué is easy when you start out with the right supplies. Cotton machine embroidery thread is easy to work with. Pick a color that matches the appliqué fabric as closely as possible. Use a long, thin needle like a sharp for stitching and slender appliqué or silk pins for holding shapes in place.

1. Make a plastic template for every shape in the appliqué design. Use a dotted line to show where pieces overlap.

2. Place template on right side of appliqué fabric. Trace around template.

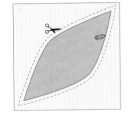

3. Cut out shapes ¼" beyond traced line.

4. Position shapes on background fabric. For pieces that overlap, follow numbers on patterns. Pieces with lower numbers go underneath; pieces with higher numbers are layered on top. Pin shapes in place.

5. Stitch shapes in order following pattern numbers. Where shapes overlap, do not turn under and stitch edges of bottom pieces. Turn and stitch the edges of the piece on top.

6. Use the traced line as your turn-under guide. Entering from the wrong side of the appliqué shape, bring the needle up on the traced line. Using the tip of the needle, turn under the fabric along the traced line. Using a blind stitch, stitch along the folded edge to join the appliqué shape to the background fabric. Turn under and stitch about ¼" at a time.

7. Clip curves and V-shapes to help the fabric turn under smoothly. Clip to within a couple threads of the traced line.

8. After stitching the entire block, place it face down on top of a thick towel and press.

QUICK CORNER TRIANGLES

Quick corner triangles are formed by simply sewing fabric squares to other squares and rectangles. The directions and diagrams with each project show you what size pieces to use and where to place square on corresponding piece. Follow steps 1–3 below to make corner triangle units.

1. With pencil and ruler, draw diagonal line on wrong side of fabric square that will form the triangle. See Diagram A. This will be your sewing line.

A.

sewing line

2. With right sides together, place square on corresponding piece. Matching raw edges, pin in place and sew ON drawn line.

B.

trim ¼" away from sewing

3. Press seam in direction of arrow as shown in step-by-step project diagram. Trim off excess fabric leaving ¼" seam allowance as shown in Diagram B. Measure completed corner triangle unit to ensure greatest accuracy.

C.

finished corner triangle unit

EMBROIDERY STITCH GUIDE

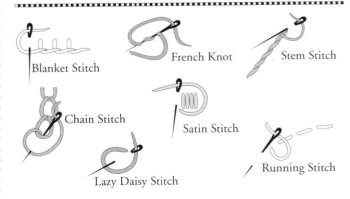

Blanket Stitch

French Knot

Stem Stitch

Chain Stitch

Satin Stitch

Lazy Daisy Stitch

Running Stitch

LAYERING THE QUILT

1. Cut backing and batting 4" to 8" larger than quilt top.

2. Lay pressed backing on bottom (right side down), batting in middle, and pressed quilt top on top. Make sure everything is centered and that backing and batting are flat. Backing and batting will extend beyond quilt top.

3. Begin basting in center and work toward outside edges. Baste vertically and horizontally, forming a 3" – 4" grid. Baste or pin completely around edge of quilt top. Quilt as desired.

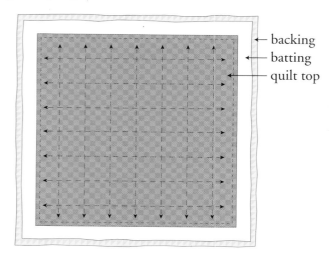

← backing
← batting
← quilt top

BINDING THE QUILT

1. Trim batting and backing to ¼" from raw edge of quilt top.

2. Fold and press binding strips in half lengthwise with wrong sides together.

3. With raw edges even, lay binding strips on top and bottom edges of quilt top. Sew through all layers, ¼" from quilt edge. Press binding away from quilt top. Trim excess length of binding.

4. Sew remaining two binding strips to quilt sides. Press and trim excess length.

5. Folding top and bottom first, fold binding around to back. Press and pin in position. Hand stitch binding in place.

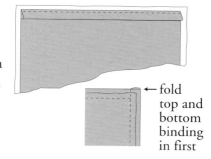

← fold top and bottom binding in first

QUICK-FUSE APPLIQUÉ

Quick-fuse appliqué is a method of adhering appliqué pieces to a background with fusible web. For quick and easy results, simply quick-fuse appliqué pieces in place. Use sewable, lightweight fusible web, for the projects in this book. Finishing raw edges with stitching is desirable. Laundering is not recommended unless edges are finished.

1. With paper side up, lay fusible web over appliqué design. Leaving ½" space between pieces, trace all elements of design. Cut around traced pieces, approximately ¼" outside traced line. See Diagram A.

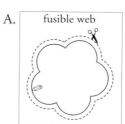

A. fusible web

2. With paper side up, position and iron fusible web to wrong side of selected fabrics. Follow manufacturer's directions for iron temperature and fusing time. Cut out each piece on traced line. See Diagram B.

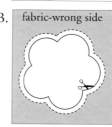

B. fabric-wrong side

3. Remove paper backing from pieces. A thin film will remain on wrong side. Position and fuse all pieces of one appliqué design at a time onto background, referring to color photos for placement.